$32⁰⁰
5/11/10

Careers in Focus

TELECOMMUNICATIONS

Ferguson
An imprint of Infobase Publishing

Careers in Focus: Telecommunications

Copyright © 2009 by Infobase Publishing

Ferguson
An imprint of Infobase Publishing
132 West 31st Street
New York NY 10001

Library of Congress Cataloging-in-Publication Data

Careers in focus. Telecommunications.
      p. cm.
 Includes bibliographical references and index.
 ISBN-13: 978-0-8160-7301-6 (alk. paper)
 ISBN-10: 0-8160-7301-5 (alk. paper)
 1. Telecommunication—Vocational guidance—Juvenile literature. 2. Telecom-munications engineers—Juvenile literature. I. Ferguson Publishing.
 TK5102.6.C37 2009
 621.382023—dc22
                                    2008037090

Ferguson books are available at special discounts when purchased in bulk quantities for businesses, associations, institutions, or sales promotions. Please call our Special Sales Department in New York at (212) 967-8800 or (800) 322-8755.

You can find Ferguson on the World Wide Web at http://www.fergpubco.com

Text design by David Strelecky
Cover design by Salvatore Luongo

Printed in the United States of America

IBT MSRF 10 9 8 7 6 5 4 3 2

This book is printed on acid-free paper.

Table of Contents

Introduction

Talking on the phone. Texting. Sending an email. Surfing the Web. Watching cable or satellite TV. These are just some of the telecommunications-related activities that you might take for granted as you go about your daily life. But go a day—or even a few hours—without your phone, Internet connection, or favorite cable channel, and you will quickly come to appreciate the importance of telecommunications professionals.

The modern telecommunications industry consists of companies that provide wired and wireless communication, Internet, and cable and satellite services. There are numerous and diverse employment opportunities available—whether you want to install fiber optic cable, design and build cutting-edge cell phone technology, help customers troubleshoot problems, teach students about telecommunications, write technical manuals and user guides, sell telecommunications products and services, or work in other specialties.

Careers in telecommunications offer a great range of earnings potential and educational requirements. Earnings range from slightly more than minimum wage to $100,000 or more for very experienced and successful college professors, engineers, designers, and marketing and sales workers. A few of these careers—such as cable television technician, customer service representative, fiber optics technician, and line installer—require a high school diploma and on-the-job training, and are excellent starting points for a career in the industry. Others, such as engineering technician, microelectronics technician, and wireless service technician, require some postsecondary training or an associate's degree. Many professional and marketing positions in the industry (such as engineer, designer, and marketing research analyst) require a minimum of a bachelor's degree. The career of college professor requires at least a master's degree. Advanced degrees—especially for science and engineering professionals—are usually required for the best positions.

Approximately 973,000 people are employed in the telecommunications industry, according to the U.S. Department of Labor. Large telecommunications companies include Qualcomm, AT&T, Verizon, Nokia, Motorola, Sony Ericsson, Comcast Cable Communications, Time Warner Cable, Cox Communications, Charter Communications, DirecTV, and Dish Network Services.

The U.S. Department of Labor predicts that employment in the telecommunications industry will increase by 5 percent through

2016—or more slowly than the average for all industries. Despite this prediction, opportunities should be good—especially in the short term—as companies build more advanced communications networks, improve the speed and reliability of the Internet and wireless networks, and offer more products and services. Once these improved systems are in place, employment may slow for workers in installation and maintenance.

Employment should be best for customer service representatives, electrical and electronics engineers, wireless sales workers, and computer support specialists. Workers with advanced training and education will have the best employment opportunities in this highly technological and rewarding field.

Each article in this book discusses a particular telecommunications industry occupation in detail. The articles in *Careers in Focus: Telecommunications* appear in Ferguson's *Encyclopedia of Careers and Vocational Guidance,* but have been updated and revised with the latest information from the U.S. Department of Labor, professional organizations, and other sources.

The following paragraphs detail the sections and features that appear in the book.

The **Quick Facts** section provides a brief summary of the career including recommended school subjects, personal skills, work environment, minimum educational requirements, salary ranges, certification or licensing requirements, and employment outlook. This section also provides acronyms and identification numbers for the following government classification indexes: the *Dictionary of Occupational Titles* (DOT), the *Guide for Occupational Exploration* (GOE), the National Occupational Classification (NOC) Index, and the Occupational Information Network (O*NET)-Standard Occupational Classification System (SOC) index. The DOT, GOE, and O*NET-SOC indexes have been created by the U.S. government; the NOC index is Canada's career classification system. Readers can use the identification numbers listed in the Quick Facts section to access further information about a career. Print editions of the DOT (*Dictionary of Occupational Titles.* Indianapolis, Ind.: JIST Works, 1991) and GOE (*Guide for Occupational Exploration.* Indianapolis, Ind.: JIST Works, 2001) are available at libraries. Electronic versions of the NOC (http://www23.hrdc-drhc.gc.ca) and O*NET-SOC (http://online.onetcenter.org) are available on the Internet. When no DOT, GOE, NOC, or O*NET-SOC numbers are present, this means that the U.S. Department of Labor or Human Resources Development Canada have not created a numerical designation for this career. In this instance, you will see the acronym "N/A," or not available.

The **Overview** section is a brief introductory description of the duties and responsibilities involved in this career. Oftentimes, a career may have a variety of job titles. When this is the case, alternative career titles are presented. Employment statistics are also provided, when available. The **History** section describes the history of the particular job as it relates to the overall development of its industry or field. **The Job** describes the primary and secondary duties of the job. **Requirements** discusses high school and postsecondary education and training requirements, any certification or licensing that is necessary, and other personal requirements for success in the job. **Exploring** offers suggestions on how to gain experience in or knowledge of the particular job before making a firm educational and financial commitment. The focus is on what can be done while still in high school (or in the early years of college) to gain a better understanding of the job. The **Employers** section gives an overview of typical places of employment for the job. **Starting Out** discusses the best ways to land that first job, be it through the college career services office, newspaper ads, Internet employment sites, or personal contact. The **Advancement** section describes what kind of career path to expect from the job and how to get there. **Earnings** lists salary ranges and describes the typical fringe benefits. The **Work Environment** section describes the typical surroundings and conditions of employment—whether indoors or outdoors, noisy or quiet, social or independent. In addition, this section discusses typical hours worked, any seasonal fluctuations, and the stresses and strains of the job. The **Outlook** section summarizes the job in terms of the general economy and industry projections. For the most part, Outlook information is obtained from the U.S. Bureau of Labor Statistics, a division of the U.S. Department of Labor, and is supplemented by information gathered from professional associations. Job growth terms follow those used in the *Occupational Outlook Handbook*. Growth described as "much faster than the average" means an increase of 21 percent or more. Growth described as "faster than the average" means an increase of 14 to 20 percent. Growth described as "about as fast as the average" means an increase of 7 to 13 percent. Growth described as "more slowly than the average" means an increase of 3 to 6 percent. "Little or no change" means a decrease of 2 percent to an increase of 2 percent. "Decline" means a decrease of 3 percent or more. Each article ends with **For More Information,** which lists organizations that provide information on training, education, internships, scholarships, and job placement.

Careers in Focus: Telecommunications also includes photographs, informative sidebars, and interviews with professionals in the field.

Cable Television Technicians

OVERVIEW

Cable television technicians install, inspect, maintain, and repair antennas, cables, and amplifying equipment used in cable television transmission. Approximately 162,000 telecommunications line installers and repairers are employed in the United States.

HISTORY

The growth of cable television transmission systems greatly affected the broadcast industry. The birth of cable television can be traced to the development of coaxial cable (copper wire inside an aluminum tube, both with the same axis), which was invented in the 1930s in the Bell Telephone Laboratories, primarily to improve telephone transmission. It was soon found that a coaxial cable could also carry television transmissions very efficiently. One coaxial cable can carry up to 500 television signals, enabling a cable system to offer a wide variety of programming and still reserve channels for public-service use.

No one knows for sure when or where the first cable television system was installed, but by 1950, early cable television systems were in use. The first cable television systems used a central receiving antenna to pick up programs from broadcast stations and were used to carry television signals to areas where conventional transmission could not reach: valleys, extremely hilly regions, and large cities where buildings interfered with radio waves. Cable systems were then built in areas with good reception as a way of offering subscribers an increased number of channels.

In the 1950s and 1960s, cable television operators began using microwave radio relays for signals. This allowed the Federal Communications Commission (FCC) to establish its authority over cable television, as the FCC regulates any use of microwave transmission systems.

Channel converters were introduced in the 1960s, allowing cable television systems to deliver a greater number of channels, and thus, a wider choice of programs. When cable television operators offered pay-TV to the public in the 1960s, there was much public outcry. The public was so accustomed to being offered TV programming at no charge that they could not accept what seemed to be an outrageous concept. California, in fact, passed a state referendum that actually outlawed pay-TV. The referendum was later overruled by the state supreme court as being unconstitutional.

The broadcast industry also opposed cable television, fearing competition in its markets. In 1968, the FCC actually forbade new cable construction in some areas. Though it later lifted this ban, it continued to restrict what cable television companies could offer the public.

In 1972, pay-TV, or pay-cable, was reintroduced by Home Box Office (HBO), which offered special programs to subscribers who paid a fee in addition to its charge for basic cable service. At first, HBO distributed its programs through a tape distribution system, then a microwave distribution network. Three years later, HBO began distributing pay-cable by satellite, which led to the rapid expansion of cable television as we know it today.

Satellites supply programming to cable television systems by relaying signals from one point on earth to another. To receive signals from a communications satellite, an earth station, or satellite receiving dish, is used. The signals are then transmitted across coaxial lines or hybrid fiber/coaxial cables to the subscriber's television.

Approximately 58 percent of households with televisions subscribe to a pay service, and for the majority of these households the service is cable television. Other pay television services, such as satellite subscriptions, are also becoming popular. Cable operators are currently upgrading their systems to offer even more services, such as digital and high-definition television (HDTV) programming, telephone communication services, and high-speed Internet access. More than 36 million cable subscribers receive digital TV. The FCC has also been involved in introducing digital television transmission. The FCC required all commercial stations to switch to an all digital broadcast system in 2009.

THE JOB

Cable television technicians perform a wide range of duties in a variety of settings. Television cables usually follow the routes of telephone cables, running along poles in rural and suburban areas and through tunnels in cities. Working in tunnels and underground cable passageways, cable television technicians inspect cables for evidence of damage and corrosion. Using diagrams and blueprints, they trace cables to locate sites of signal breakdown. Technicians may also work at pole-mounted amplifiers, where they analyze the strength of incoming television signals, using field-strength meters and miniature television receivers to evaluate reception. At customers' homes, technicians service the terminal boxes, explain the workings of the cable system, answer questions, and respond to complaints that may indicate cable or equipment problems. When major problems arise, they repair or replace damaged or faulty cable systems.

John Manaro works as a technician for Comcast in Santa Ana, California. He's had years of experience as both a maintenance technician and a construction technician. As a construction technician, his work has involved expanding underground service by the trenching and boring of grass, dirt, asphalt, and concrete as well as the coordination of city and county projects. As a maintenance technician, John maintained a cable television plant in three cities within a seven-city system. "I was required to maintain a level of performance and picture quality," he says, "set by system, industry, and FCC proof of performance specifications standards." To do so, Manaro followed a routine of preventive maintenance procedures. "This included the sweep and balance of all receivers and amplifiers in the system and operational checks and periodic tests of all power supply units. Also, I was required by the FCC to furnish documentation of all signal leakage detected in my area including corrective actions taken and dates of occurrence and correction." He was also required to perform "on-call" duties once a month for seven days. "This required response, within 30 minutes, to any outage consisting of five or more subscribers at any time, 24 hours a day."

Cable television technicians use various electrical measuring instruments (voltmeters, field-strength meters) to diagnose causes of transmission problems. They also use electricians' hand tools (including screwdrivers, pliers, etc.) to dismantle, repair, or replace faulty sections of cable or disabled equipment, such as amplifying equipment used to boost the signal at intervals along the cable system.

Some cable television technicians may perform a specific type of work, rather than a full range of tasks. Following are some of the specialized positions held by cable television technicians.

Trunk technicians, or *line technicians,* perform routine maintenance and fix electronic problems on the trunk line, which connects the feeder lines in the street to the headend. They also fix electronic failures in the feeder amplifiers. Amplifiers increase the strength of the electronic signal for clear reception and are spaced throughout the cable system. Some trunk technicians install both underground and aboveground cables. Using a sweep analyzer, they check signals in all parts of the cable television system to make sure all parts are operating correctly.

Headend technicians and *microwave technicians* check that the equipment providing input to the cable television system is working properly. The headend, or control center of a cable television system, is where incoming signals are amplified, converted, processed, and combined into a common cable. Headend technicians check antennas, preamplifiers, frequency converters, processors, demodulators, modulators, and other related equipment using power meters, frequency counters, and waveform monitors. In some companies, the headend technician works with satellite receiving stations and related equipment. This person may be the *chief technician* in some companies. Many *electronics technicians* work as headend technicians and microwave technicians

Service technicians respond to problems with subscribers' cable reception. They work on amplifiers, poles, and lines, in addition to making calls to subscribers' homes. They check the lines and connections that go into a home and those inside it, troubleshoot problems, and repair faulty equipment.

Bench technicians work in a cable television system's repair facility. They examine malfunctioning equipment that is brought into the shop, diagnose the problem, and repair it. They may also repair and calibrate test equipment. Some bench technicians are electronics technicians.

Technical supervisors oversee the technicians who work in the field and provide on-the-job training to technicians. Duties vary but can include dealing with contractors and coordinating with outside agencies such as utility companies, municipalities, and large customers.

Chief technicians and *lead technicians* are among the most highly skilled of the technical staff. Many chief technicians do not work in the field except in emergency situations or complex situations requiring their special expertise. Chief technicians provide technical information to technicians in the field and may supervise the technical

Top Cable Companies by Subscriber Count

	Total Subscribers
1. Comcast Cable Communications	24,156,000
2. Time Warner Cable	13,308,000
3. Cox Communications	5,414,000
4. Charter Communications	5,347,800
5. Cablevision Systems	3,122,000
6. Bright House Networks LLC	2,329,400
7. Mediacom LLC	1,331,000
8. Suddenlink Communications	1,290,000
9. Insight Communications	722,000
10. CableOne	701,900

Source: SNL Kagan, September 2007

staff. They may work with satellite receiving equipment. These positions are usually held by senior staff personnel and require a strong background in electronics.

An important aspect of the work of cable television technicians involves implementing regular programs of preventive maintenance on the cable system. Technicians inspect connections, insulation, and the performance of amplifying equipment, using measuring instruments and viewing the transmitted signals on television monitors.

REQUIREMENTS

High School
You should take high school mathematics courses at least through plane geometry and have a solid knowledge of shop mathematics. You should also take English classes to develop the language skills needed to read technical manuals and instructions and to follow detailed maintenance procedures.

Postsecondary Training
Although training beyond high school is not required, many employers prefer to hire applicants with an electronics background or people

who have had some technical training. Technical training in electronics technology or communications technology is available through both one- and two-year programs at community colleges, trade schools, and technical institutes. Two-year programs provide hands-on training and include courses that cover the basics of electrical wiring and electronics, broadcasting theory and practice, blueprint and schematic diagram reading, and physics. JONES/NCTI offers online and distance-learning courses for technicians.

Certification or Licensing

Certification in special skills can be obtained through one-year certification programs at community colleges. Certification classes in specialized technology, such as digital technology, digital compression, and fiber optics, prepare students to work with the more advanced technologies commonly used in many cable television systems. Because cable technology is evolving so rapidly, students who learn new technology have better chances at employment, and once hired, they have better chances for advancement. All workers are encouraged to continue training throughout their careers to learn new technology, new equipment, and new methods.

Professional associations, such as the Society of Cable Telecommunications Engineers (SCTE), also offer training programs and certification in areas, such as broadband communications technology. Examinations for certification are offered in different areas of cable technology including video and audio signals and systems, signal processing centers, terminal devices, and data networking and architecture. The Telecommunications Industry Association offers a certification program for technicians working in convergence technologies and the International Association for Radio, Telecommunications and Electromagnetics offers certification for technicians employed in the telecommunications industry.

Other Requirements

You'll need mechanical aptitude, physical agility, the ability to work at heights or in confined spaces, and the capacity to work as part of a team. Acute vision, with no color-perception deficiency, is needed, as it is essential for analyzing cable reception. In addition, it is helpful to feel at ease in using electrical equipment and electricians' tools. "I have a desire for knowledge," John Manaro says about the personal qualities that make him good at his work, "and a dedication to perfection. And I'm detail oriented."

You'll have much public contact, so you'll need good people skills. You must be helpful and courteous. You may need to explain cable system operations and costs to customers, answer questions, and analyze customer descriptions of problems so repairs and other work can be done. The ability to communicate well with others is essential.

EXPLORING

Because of the special training required, rarely are any part-time or summer technician jobs available for high school students. However, educational seminars are offered by local cable television personnel across the country; these are available to interested student groups and can be arranged through a school guidance counselor or teacher. These presentations provide valuable career information and an opportunity to speak with cable technicians and their employers about the field. For more information about these seminars, contact the SCTE for the name and address of the nearest local chapter.

Those interested in this career can explore electronics or related activities such as building a shortwave radio set or repairing radios and televisions, and participate in science clubs that emphasize electronics.

EMPLOYERS

Approximately 162,000 telecommunications line installers and repairers are employed in the United States. Cable television technicians work for cable-TV companies in large cities and small towns. Some smaller towns may have only one cable provider, while there may be more than one in large cities. Technicians may work for a locally owned company or for the local office of a large, national corporation, such as Cox Communications. The company may offer services in addition to cable television, such as Internet access and local telephone service.

STARTING OUT

Two ways to enter this field are as an unskilled installer and move up after receiving on-the-job training or to complete an electronics or telecommunications program in a technical school or through the SCTE and start work as an electronics technician or cable television technician. Many times, recruiters from various companies visit technical schools or hold job fairs in which they interview students for positions that begin immediately after training has been completed. Students can also check with their schools' career services office for postings by employers or to get leads on companies that are hiring.

State employment offices and classified ads are other good sources of job leads. Interested persons also can apply directly to a cable television company or contractor.

ADVANCEMENT

Most companies provide on-the-job training, including classes in basic technical and troubleshooting skills, basic electronics, and electronics in reference to the cable television business, parts of the cable television system, installation, and safety practices. Students who have already received technical training usually are able to advance into more highly skilled positions more quickly than those who require extensive training. Many cable television technicians start out as installers or repairers and then move into technical positions, such as line technician, service technician, and bench technician. Workers with a strong industrial background, advanced training in electronics, and several years of experience can advance to supervisory and administrative positions, such as *technical supervisor, headend technician, chief technician, lead technician,* and *plant manager.*

Workers also can advance to the position of *chief engineer* with additional training. Chief engineers are responsible for cable systems design, equipment planning, specification of standards for equipment and material, layout for cable communications networks, and technical advice to technicians and system operating managers. A degree in electrical engineering or a related field is required to be a chief engineer.

"I hope to remain a field-oriented person," John Manaro says, "in either the cable or telecommunications industry. More and more, I see that this is the area where you can never become obsolete."

EARNINGS

According to the U.S. Department of Labor, the mean annual pay for nonsupervisory cable and other pay television installers and repairers was $38,800 in 2006 for full-time work. Salaries, however, vary based on the type of job done, an employee's experience and education, and the company's location. At the low end of the pay scale, 10 percent of all line installers and repairers had annual earnings of less than $24,700 annually, while at the high end, 10 percent earned more than $68,220.

Cable television technicians may receive a variety of benefits, depending on their employer. The benefits can include any of the following: paid holidays, vacations, and sick days; personal days; medical, dental, and life insurance; profit-sharing plans; 401(k) plans; retirement and pension plans; and educational assistance programs.

WORK ENVIRONMENT

The work is moderately heavy, involving occasional lifting of up to 50 pounds. A large part of the cable television technician's time is spent on ladders and poles or in confined or underground spaces. These activities require care and precision. As with all maintenance work around conductors, there is some danger of electrical shock. The coaxial cables used to transmit television signals are from one-half inch to over one inch in diameter. Cables have to be manipulated into position for splicing, which involves medium to heavy physical work.

Normal working hours are a five-day, 40-hour week, although technicians may often need to work evenings or weekends to make necessary repairs. Some technicians work in shifts, working four 10-hour days a week. Many technicians, especially line technicians, are on call 24 hours a day and carry pagers. They may be called in for special repairs or in emergency situations.

Technicians working in the field work in all kinds of weather. Their work involves extensive driving. Most companies provide a company vehicle, tools, equipment, and sometimes uniforms. "A job in the field is very demanding," John Manaro says. "Not just physically, but intellectually and emotionally. It can be very stressful. Maintaining a system requires real dedication and perseverance and can consume a great deal of time and energy."

OUTLOOK

Employment for cable television technicians is expected to grow more slowly than the average for all occupations through 2014, according to the U.S. Department of Labor. Despite this prediction, there should continue to be openings for new technicians as existing technicians retire. Cable companies will continue to need technicians to install additional fiber optic cables, work with new technologies that increase cable line capacities and capabilities, and maintain the systems. Those with strong technical skills should have the best employment opportunities.

Growth will be tempered by an increasing trend toward the use of wireless technology and satellite technology, as well as productivity gains that will allow fewer employees to do more work.

FOR MORE INFORMATION

For technician training course information, contact
Jones/NCTI
9697 East Mineral Avenue
Centennial, CO 80112-3408

Tel: 866-575-7206
http://www.jonesncti.com

For information on certification, contact
International Association for Radio, Telecommunications and
Electromagnetics
840 Queen Street
New Bern, NC 28560-4856
Tel: 800-89-NARTE
http://www.narte.org

For information on careers and the cable industry, contact
National Cable & Telecommunications Association
25 Massachusetts Avenue, NW, Suite 100
Washington, DC 20001-1434
Tel: 202-222-2300
http://www.ncta.com

*For information on careers, educational programs, educational
seminars, distance learning, and certification, contact*
Society of Cable Telecommunications Engineers
140 Philips Road
Exton, PA 19341-1318
Tel: 800-542-5040
Email: scte@scte.org
http://www.scte.org

For information on certification, contact
Telecommunications Industry Association
2500 Wilson Boulevard, Suite 300
Arlington, VA 22201-3834
Tel: 703-907-7700
http://www.tiaonline.org

*For information about conferences, special programs, careers, and
membership, contact*
Women in Cable Telecommunications
14555 Avion Parkway, Suite 250
Chantilly, VA 20151-1117
Tel: 703-234-9810
http://www.wict.org

College Professors, Telecommunications

OVERVIEW

College professors instruct undergraduate and graduate students in telecommunications-related subjects at colleges and universities. They lecture classes, lead small seminar groups, and create and grade examinations. They also may conduct research, write for publication, and aid in administration.

HISTORY

In the early days of the telecommunications industry most workers received their training on the job or through apprenticeships. Advanced workers, such as engineers and scientists, trained for the field by earning traditional degrees in engineering or science and acquiring knowledge about the industry through on-the-job experience, military training, or through telecommunications-related classes. It was not until the last several decades—in response to the growing complexity and diversity of telecommunications systems (including telephones, cell phones, cable and video technology, and the Internet)—that colleges and universities began creating separate programs (or expanding existing engineering and computer science programs) in order to prepare telecommunications workers. With nearly one million workers in the field today, and technology constantly changing, there is growing demand for telecommunications teachers to prepare future telecommunications engineers, scientists, technicians, and other workers in the field.

THE JOB

College and university faculty members teach at junior colleges or at four-year colleges and universities. At four-year institutions, most faculty members are *assistant professors, associate professors,* or *full professors.* These three types of professorships differ in regards to status, job responsibilities, and salary. Assistant professors are new faculty members who are working to get tenure (status as a permanent professor); they seek to advance to associate and then to full professorships.

Telecommunications professors perform three main functions: teaching, advising, and research. Their most important responsibility is to teach students. Their role within a college department will determine the level of courses they teach and the number of courses per semester. Most professors work with students at all levels, from college freshmen to graduate students. They may head several classes a semester or only a few a year. Some of their classes will have large enrollment, while graduate seminars may consist of only 12 or fewer students. Though college telecommunications professors may spend fewer than 15 hours a week in the actual classroom, they spend many hours preparing lectures and lesson plans, grading papers and exams, and preparing grade reports. They also schedule office hours during the week to be available to students outside of the lecture hall, and they meet with students individually throughout the semester. In the classroom, professors lecture, lead discussions, administer exams, and assign textbook reading and other research. While most professors teach entry-level classes such as Introduction to Fiber Optics, Database Systems, and Programming for Telecommunications, some also teach higher-level classes, such as Advanced Software Engineering, Advanced Data Structures, Remote Access Networks, Emerging Broadband Technologies, Emerging Wireless Technologies, Voice-Over IP Technologies, Solid State Devices and Circuits, Signal Transmission for Telecommunications, Data Transmission Systems, and Microcomputer Hardware. In some courses, they rely heavily on laboratories to transmit course material.

Another important responsibility is advising students. Not all faculty members serve as advisers, but those who do must set aside large blocks of time to guide students through the program. College telecommunications professors who serve as advisers may have any number of students assigned to them, from fewer than 10 to more than 100, depending on the administrative policies of the college. Their responsibility may involve looking over a planned program of studies to make sure the students meet requirements for graduation, or it may involve working intensively with each student on many aspects of college life.

The third responsibility of telecommunications faculty members is research and publication. Faculty members who are heavily involved in research programs sometimes are assigned a smaller teaching load. Telecommunications professors publish their research findings in various trade and scholarly journals such as *IEEE Wireless Communication Magazine, Communications Technology, Optics & Photonics News*, and *Wireless Week*. They also write books based on their research or on their own knowledge and experience in the field. Most textbooks are written by college and university teachers.

Publishing a significant amount of work has been the traditional standard by which assistant telecommunications professors prove themselves worthy of becoming permanent, tenured faculty. Typically, pressure to publish is greatest for assistant professors. Pressure to publish increases again if an associate professor wishes to be considered for a promotion to full professorship. Professors in junior colleges face less pressure to publish than those in four-year institutions.

Some telecommunications faculty members eventually rise to the position of *department chair*, where they govern the affairs of an entire department. Department chairs, faculty, and other professional staff members are aided in their myriad duties by *graduate assistants,* who may help develop teaching materials, conduct research, give examinations, teach lower-level courses, and carry out other activities such as grading papers and exams.

Some telecommunications professors may also conduct classes in an extension program. In such a program, they teach evening and weekend courses for the benefit of people who otherwise would not be able to take advantage of the institution's resources. They may travel away from the campus and meet with a group of students at another location. They may work full time for the extension division or may divide their time between on-campus and off-campus teaching.

Distance learning programs, an increasingly popular option for students, give telecommunications professors the opportunity to use today's technologies to remain in one place while teaching students who are at a variety of locations simultaneously. The professor's duties, like those when teaching correspondence courses conducted by mail, include grading work that students send in at periodic intervals and advising students of their progress. Computers, the Internet, email, and video conferencing, however, are some of the technology tools that allow professors and students to communicate in "real time" in a virtual classroom setting. Meetings may be scheduled during the same time as traditional classes or during evenings and weekends. Professors who do this work are sometimes known as *extension work, correspondence,* or *distance learning instructors.* They may teach online courses in addition to other classes or may have distance learning as their major teaching responsibility.

The *junior college telecommunications instructor* has many of the same kinds of responsibilities as does the teacher in a four-year college or university. Because junior colleges offer only a two-year program, they teach only undergraduates.

REQUIREMENTS

High School
Your high school's college preparatory program likely includes courses in English, science, foreign language, history, math, and government. In addition, you should take courses in speech to get a sense of what it will be like to lecture to a group of students. Your school's debate team can also help you develop public speaking skills, along with research skills.

Postsecondary Training
At least one advanced degree in telecommunications or a related field (such as information systems, hardware engineering, software engineering, fiber optics, computer network administration, electrical or electronics engineering/technology, information security, or wireless networking) is required to be a professor in a college or university. Typical classes focus on telecommunications technology, repair, networking, software, emerging technologies, and management. The master's degree is considered the minimum standard, and graduate work beyond the master's is usually desirable. If you hope to advance in academic rank above instructor, most institutions require a doctorate. Only a few colleges offer graduate degrees in telecommunications; you will have to earn a graduate degree in engineering or a related field and minor or take a concentration in telecommunications.

In the last year of your undergraduate program, you'll apply to graduate programs in your area of study. Standards for admission to a graduate program can be high and the competition heavy, depending on the school. Once accepted into a program, your responsibilities will be similar to those of your professors—in addition to attending seminars, you will conduct research, prepare articles for publication, and teach some undergraduate courses.

You may find employment in a junior college with only a master's degree. Advancement in responsibility and in salary, however, is more likely to come if you have earned a doctorate.

Other Requirements

You should enjoy reading, writing, and researching. Not only will you spend many years studying in school, but your whole career will be based on communicating your thoughts and ideas. People skills are important because you'll be dealing directly with students, administrators, and other faculty members on a daily basis. You should feel comfortable in a role of authority and possess self-confidence.

EXPLORING

Your high school teachers use many of the same skills as college professors, so talk to your teachers about their careers and their college experiences. You can develop your own teaching experience by volunteering at a community center, working at a day care center, or working at a summer camp. Also, spend some time on a college campus to get a sense of the environment. Write to colleges for their admissions brochures and course catalogs (or check them out online); read about the telecommunications faculty members and the courses they teach. Before visiting college campuses, make arrangements to speak to professors who teach courses that interest you. These professors may allow you to sit in on their classes and observe. Also, make appointments with college advisers and with people in the admissions and recruitment offices. If your grades are good enough, you might be able to serve as a teaching assistant during your undergraduate years, which can give you experience leading discussions and grading papers.

EMPLOYERS

Employment opportunities vary based on area of study and education. Most universities have many different departments that hire telecommunications faculty including computer science and engineering. Some colleges also have stand-alone telecommunications departments. With a doctorate, a number of publications, and a record of good teaching, professors should find opportunities in universities all across the country. Professors teach in undergraduate and graduate programs. The teaching jobs at doctoral institutions are usually better paying and more prestigious. The most sought-after positions are those that offer tenure. Teachers that have only a master's degree will be limited to opportunities with junior colleges, community colleges, and some small private institutions.

STARTING OUT

You should start the process of finding a teaching position while you are in graduate school. The process includes developing a curriculum vitae (a detailed, academic resume), writing for publication, assisting with research, attending conferences, and gaining teaching experience and recommendations. Many students begin applying for teaching positions while finishing their graduate program. For most positions at four-year institutions, you must travel to large conferences where interviews can be arranged with representatives from the universities to which you have applied.

Because of the competition for tenure-track positions, you may have to work for a few years in temporary positions, visiting various schools as an adjunct professor. Some professional associations maintain lists of teaching opportunities in their areas. They may also make lists of applicants available to college administrators looking to fill an available position.

ADVANCEMENT

The normal pattern of advancement is from instructor to assistant professor, to associate professor, to full professor. All four academic ranks are concerned primarily with teaching and research. College faculty members who have an interest in and a talent for administration may be advanced to chair of a department or to dean of their college. A few become college or university presidents or other types of administrators.

The instructor is usually an inexperienced college teacher. He or she may hold a doctorate or may have completed all the Ph.D. requirements except for the dissertation. Most colleges look upon the rank of instructor as the period during which the college is trying out the teacher. Instructors usually are advanced to the position of assistant professors within three to four years. Assistant professors are given up to about six years to prove themselves worthy of tenure, and if they do so, they become associate professors. Some professors choose to remain at the associate level. Others strive to become full professors and receive greater status, salary, and responsibilities.

Most colleges have clearly defined promotion policies for faculty members. Many colleges and universities have written statements

Facts about the Telecommunications Industry, 2006

- Approximately 973,000 people were employed in the industry.
- Wired telecommunications carriers employed 49 percent of workers; wireless telecommunications carriers, 21 percent; cable and other program distributors, 15 percent; and satellite telecommunications and telecommunications resellers, 15 percent.
- More than 50 percent of telecommunications professionals worked at establishments that employed between five and 249 workers.
- The average annual earnings of nonsupervisory workers in the industry were $50,076.
- Twenty-two percent of workers were members of a union—9 percent higher than the average for all workers.

Source: U.S. Department of Labor

about the number of years in which instructors and assistant professors may remain at their present academic rank before applying for tenure or a promotion to the next tenured level at the institution. If an instructor or an assistant professor does not obtain a tenured faculty position at their college or university within a specified period of time, he or she will be encouraged or required to seek another faculty position at a different college or university. Administrators in many colleges hope to encourage younger faculty members to increase their skills and competencies and thus to qualify for the more responsible and prestigious positions of associate professor and full professor.

EARNINGS

Earnings vary by the departments professors work in, by the size of the school, by the type of school (public, private, women's only, for example), and by the level of position the professor holds. In its 2006-07 salary survey, the American Association of University Professors reported the average yearly income for all full-time faculty was $73,207. It also reports that professors earned the following average salaries by rank: full professors, $98,974; associate professors, $69,911; assistant professors, $58,662; instructors, $42,609; and lecturers, $48,289.

According to the U.S. Department of Labor, in 2006, the median salary for all postsecondary instructors was $63,930, with 10 percent earning $120,580 or more and 10 percent earning $33,590 or less. Those with the highest earnings tend to be senior tenured faculty; those with the lowest, graduate assistants. Professors working on the West Coast and the East Coast and those working at doctorate-granting institutions also tend to have the highest salaries. Many professors try to increase their earnings by completing research, publishing in their field, or teaching additional courses.

Benefits for full-time telecommunications faculty typically include health insurance and retirement funds and, in some cases, stipends for travel related to research, housing allowances, and tuition waivers for dependents.

WORK ENVIRONMENT

A college or university is usually a pleasant place in which to work. Campuses bustle with all types of activities and events, stimulating ideas, and a young, energetic population. Much prestige comes with success as a telecommunications professor and scholar; professors have the respect of students, colleagues, and others in their community.

Depending on the size of the department, telecommunications professors may have their own office, or they may have to share an office with one or more colleagues. Their department may provide them with a computer, Internet access, and research assistants. College professors are also able to do much of their office work at home. They can arrange their schedule around class hours, academic meetings, and the established office hours when they meet with students. Most telecommunications teachers work more than 40 hours each week. Although college professors may teach only two or three classes a semester, they spend many hours preparing for lectures, examining student work, and conducting research.

OUTLOOK

Overall employment in the telecommunications industry is expected to grow more slowly than the average for all industries through 2016, according to the U.S. Department of Labor. Employment areas that are expected to show the strongest growth include wireless technology, electronics engineering, computer science, sales and marketing, and customer service. Professors who teach classes in these fields should have good employment opportunities.

The U.S. Department of Labor predicts much faster than average employment growth for college and university professors through 2016. College enrollment is projected to grow due to an increased number of 18- to 24-year-olds, an increased number of adults returning to college, and an increased number of foreign-born students. Retirement of current faculty members will also provide job openings. However, competition for full-time, tenure-track positions at four-year schools will be very strong.

FOR MORE INFORMATION

To read about the issues affecting college professors, contact the following organizations:

American Association of University Professors
1012 14th Street, NW, Suite 500
Washington, DC 20005-3406
Tel: 202-737-5900
Email: aaup@aaup.org
http://www.aaup.org

American Federation of Teachers
555 New Jersey Avenue, NW
Washington, DC 20001-2029
Tel: 202-879-4400
Email: online@aft.org
http://www.aft.org

For information on internships, student membership, and the student magazine, Crossroads, *contact*

Association for Computing Machinery
1515 Broadway
New York, NY 10036-8901
Tel: 212-869-7440
http://www.acm.org

To learn about fiber optics, contact

Fiber Optic Association
1119 South Mission Road, #355
Fallbrook, CA 92028-3225
Tel: 760-451-3655
Email: info@thefoa.org
http://www.thefoa.org

For information on scholarships, student membership, and to read Careers in Computer Science and Computer Engineering, *visit the IEEE's Web site.*

IEEE Computer Society
1828 L Street, NW, Suite 1202

Washington, DC 20036-5104
Tel: 202-371-0101
http://www.computer.org

For information on careers and educational programs, contact
Institute of Electrical and Electronics Engineers
1828 L Street, NW, Suite 1202
Washington, DC 20036-5104
Tel: 202-785-0017
Email: ieeeusa@ieee.org
http://www.ieee.org

For information on careers and the cable industry, contact
National Cable & Telecommunications Association
25 Massachusetts Avenue, NW, Suite 100
Washington, DC 20001-1434
Tel: 202-222-2300
http://www.ncta.com

To learn about telecommunications technology and uses for fiber optics, visit the OSA Web site.
Optical Society of America (OSA)
2010 Massachusetts Avenue, NW
Washington, DC 20036-1012
Tel: 202-223-8130
Email: info@osa.org
http://www.osa.org

For information on careers and educational programs, contact
Society of Cable Telecommunications Engineers
140 Philips Road
Exton, PA 19341-1318
Tel: 800-542-5040
Email: scte@scte.org
http://www.scte.org

INTERVIEW

Warren Koontz, professor and chair of the Telecommunications Engineering Technology Program at Rochester Institute of Technology in Rochester, New York, discussed his career and the education of telecommunications engineering students with the editors of Careers in Focus: Telecommunications.

Q. Can you tell us about your program and your background?

A. The College of Applied Science and Technology at Rochester Institute of Technology (RIT) offers certificate programs, a bachelor of science, and a master of science in Telecommunications Engineering Technology (TET). The undergraduate TET Program is one of three engineering technology programs offered by the department, and each of these programs is based on a foundation of math, physics, circuit theory, electronics, and programming, as well as liberal arts. (Visit http://www.rit.edu/cast/ectet to learn more about the program.)

   I have been a professor at RIT since December 2000 and am currently a tenured full professor and chair of the TET program. Prior to coming to RIT, I was employed for more than 32 years by Bell Laboratories, where I retired as director of the Optical Networking Product Development Laboratory in Nuremberg, Germany. I have a bachelor of science from the University of Maryland, a master of science from Massachusetts Institute of Technology, and a Ph.D. from Purdue University, all in electrical engineering.

Q. What are some of the pros and cons of being a college professor?

A. The number one benefit is working with students and helping them learn. Most students are eager to learn and they actually help keep you feeling young. I also enjoy the flexible working arrangements, especially the summer break. My colleagues are great to work with and the campus is a tremendous facility for teaching, scholarship, recreation, and entertainment. My only frustration is with the complex and inefficient process for recruiting new faculty.

Q. What is one thing that young people may not know about a career in telecommunications?

A. I suspect that many do not realize how broad the field of telecommunication really is. Depending on their background, they may think that it just involves working at a telephone company or with the Internet.

Q. What are the most important personal and professional qualities for telecommunications engineering technology students?

A. They should have a good basis in fundamental subjects that will serve them for the long run. They should realize that most of the technology they will work with over the course of their careers has not been discovered yet. They also need to learn how to work in teams. All of the telecommunication problems that can be solved by a single individual have already been solved.

Q. What advice would you give students as they graduate and look for jobs?

A. Try to learn as much as you can about the variety of jobs that are available. The industry includes service providers, equipment providers, and consulting engineering firms. You may consider the large, well-known companies such as AT&T, Verizon, and Time Warner, but there are many smaller companies that have survived the "bubble" and are doing quite well. I recently spoke with the president of a telecommunications consulting company whose 150 or so employees are managing the operations of some of the largest service providers in the nation.

Q. Are there any changes in this job market that students should expect? Have certain areas of this field been especially promising in recent years?

A. They should expect change, period. VoIP (Voice over Internet Protocol) and network convergence are current buzzwords, and it is probably a good idea to be conversant in these areas.

Communications Equipment Technicians

OVERVIEW

Communications equipment technicians install, test, maintain, troubleshoot, and repair a wide variety of telephone and radio equipment used to transmit communications—voices and data—across long distances. This does not include, however, equipment that handles entertainment broadcast to the public via radio or television signals. Most communications equipment technicians work in telecommunications company offices or on customers' premises. In the United States, approximately 198,000 people work as communications equipment technicians.

HISTORY

Alexander Graham Bell patented the first practical telephone in 1876. By 1878, a commercial telephone company that switched calls between its local customers was operating in New Haven, Connecticut. For many years, telephone connections were made by operators who worked at central offices of telephone companies. A company customer who wanted to speak with another customer had to call the operator at a central office, and the operator would connect the two customer lines together by inserting a metal plug into a socket.

Today, automatic switching equipment has replaced operators for routine connections like this, and telephones are carrying much more than voice messages between local customers. Vast quantities of information are sent across phone lines in the form of visual images, computer data, and tele-

QUICK FACTS

School Subjects
Mathematics
Technical/shop

Personal Skills
Following instructions
Mechanical/manipulative

Work Environment
Primarily indoors
Primarily multiple locations

Minimum Education Level
Some postsecondary training

Salary Range
$31,110 to $50,000 to $68,310+

Certification or Licensing
Required for certain positions

Outlook
Little or no change

DOT
822

GOE
05.02.01

NOC
7246

O*NET-SOC
49-2022.00, 49-2022.03

typewriter signals. Furthermore, telephone systems today are part of larger interconnected telecommunications systems. These systems link together telephones with other equipment that sends information via microwave and television transmissions, fiber optics cables, undersea cables, and signals bounced off satellites in space. High-speed computerized switching and routing equipment makes it possible for telecommunications systems to handle millions of calls and other data signals at the same time.

THE JOB

Although specific duties vary, most communications equipment technicians share some basic kinds of activities. They work with electrical measuring and testing devices and hand tools; read blueprints, circuit diagrams, and electrical schematics (diagrams); and consult technical manuals. The following paragraphs describe just a few of the many technicians who work in this complex industry.

Central office equipment installers, also called equipment installation technicians, are specialists in setting up and taking down the switching and dialing equipment located in telephone company central offices. They install equipment in newly established offices, update existing equipment, add on to facilities that are being expanded, and remove old, outdated apparatus.

Central office repairers, also called switching equipment technicians or central office technicians, work on the switching equipment that automatically connects lines when customers dial calls. They analyze defects and malfunctions in equipment, make fine adjustments, and test and repair switches and relays. These workers use various special tools, gauges, meters, and ordinary hand tools.

PBX systems technicians or switching equipment technicians work on PBXs, or private branch exchanges, which are direct lines that businesses install to bypass phone company lines. PBX systems can handle both voice and data communications and can provide specialized services such as electronic mail and automatic routing of calls at the lowest possible cost.

PBX installers install these systems. They may assemble customized switchboards for customers. PBX repairers maintain and repair PBX systems and associated equipment. In addition, they may work on mobile radiophones and microwave transmission devices.

Maintenance administrators test customers' lines within the central office to find causes and locations of malfunctions reported by customers. They report the nature of the trouble to maintenance crews and coordinate their activities to clear up the trouble. Some maintenance administrators work in cable television company offices, diagnosing subscribers' problems with cable television signals and dispatching repairers if necessary. They use highly automated testboards and other equipment to analyze circuits. They enter data into computer files and interpret computer output about trouble areas in the system.

Many workers in this group are concerned with other kinds of communications equipment that are not part of telephone systems. Among these are *radio repairers and mechanics,* who install and repair radio transmitters and receivers. Sometimes they work on other electronics equipment at microwave and fiber optics installations. *Submarine cable equipment technicians* work on the machines and equipment used to send messages through underwater cables. Working in cable offices and stations, they check and adjust transmitters and printers and repair or replace faulty parts. *Office electricians* maintain submarine cable circuits and rearrange connections to ensure that cable service is not interrupted. *Avionics technicians* work on electronic components in aircraft communication, navigation, and flight control systems. *Signal maintainers* or *track switch maintainers* work on railroads. They install, inspect, and maintain the signals, track switches, gate crossings, and communications systems throughout rail networks. *Instrument repairers* work in repair shops, where they repair, test, and modify a variety of communications equipment.

REQUIREMENTS

High School
Most employers prefer to hire candidates with at least some postsecondary training in electronics. So to prepare for this career, you should take computer courses, algebra, geometry, English, physics, and shop classes in high school. Useful shop courses are those that introduce you to principles of electricity and electronics, basic machine repair, reading blueprints and engineering drawings, and using hand tools.

Postsecondary Training
Most telecommunications employers prefer to hire technicians who have already learned most of the necessary skills, so consider getting training in this area either through service in the military or from a postsecondary training program. Programs at community or junior colleges or technical schools in telecommunications technology, electronics, electrical, or electromechanical technology, or even computer maintenance or related subjects, may be appropriate for people who want to become communications equipment technicians.

Most programs last two years, although certification in specific areas often can be obtained through a one-year program. Useful classes are those that provide practical knowledge about electricity and electronics and teach the use of hand tools, electronic testing equipment, and computer data terminals. Classes in digital and fiber optic technology are also beneficial.

Applicants for entry-level positions may have to pass tests of their knowledge, general mechanical aptitude, and manual dexterity. Once hired, employees often go through company training programs. They may study practical and theoretical aspects of electricity, electronics, and mathematics that they will need to know for their work. Experienced workers also may attend training sessions from time to time. They need to keep their knowledge up to date as new technology in the rapidly changing telecommunications field affects the way they do their jobs.

Certification or Licensing

Some workers in this field must obtain a license. Federal Communications Commission regulations require that anyone who works with radio transmitting equipment must have a Global Maritime Distress and Safety System license. In order to receive a license, applicants need to pass a written test on radio laws and operating procedures and take a Morse code examination.

Certification for technicians is available from the International Association for Radio, Telecommunications and Electromagnetics; the Society of Cable Telecommunications Engineers; and the Telecommunications Industry Association. To receive certification, you'll need a certain amount of education and experience in telecommunications, and you'll have to pass an examination.

Other Requirements

You'll need strong mechanical and electrical aptitudes, as well as manual dexterity. Keep in mind, too, that you will be required to distinguish between colors because many wires are color-coded. You should also have problem-solving abilities and the ability to work without a lot of direct supervision. Math and computer skills are also very important; you'll also need to be able to interpret very technical manuals and blueprints. You'll be expected to keep accurate records, so you'll need to be organized.

EXPLORING

In high school, you can begin to find out about the work of communications equipment technicians by taking whatever electronics, computer, and electrical shop courses are available, and also other shop courses that help you become familiar with using various tools. Teachers or guidance counselors may be able to help you arrange a visit to a telephone company central office, where you can see telephone equipment and observe workers on the job. It may be possible to obtain a part-time or summer-helper job at a business that sells and repairs electronics equipment. Such a job could provide the opportunity to talk to workers whose skills are similar to those needed by many communications equipment technicians. Serving in the armed forces in a communications section can also provide a way to learn about this field and gain some useful experience.

EMPLOYERS

Approximately 198,000 people work as communications equipment technicians in the United States. Local and long-distance telephone companies and manufacturers of telephone and other electronic communications equipment employ communications equipment technicians. Work is also available with electrical repair shops and cable television companies.

STARTING OUT

Beginning technicians can apply directly to the employment office of the local telephone company. Many times it is necessary for newly hired workers to take a position in a different part of the company until an opening as a technician becomes available.

Books to Read

Dodd, Annabel Z. *The Essential Guide to Telecommunications.* 4th ed. Upper Saddle River, N.J.: Prentice Hall PTR, 2005.

Goleniewski, Lillian, and Kitty Wilson Jarrett. *Telecommunications Essentials: The Complete Global Source.* 2d ed. Upper Saddle River, N.J.: Addison-Wesley Professional, 2006.

Green, James Harry. *The Irwin Handbook of Telecommunications.* 5th ed. New York: McGraw-Hill, 2005.

Newton, Harry. *Newton's Telecom Dictionary: Covering Telecommunications, Networking, Information Technology, Computing and the Internet.* San Francisco: CMP Books, 2004.

Olejniczak, Stephen P. *Telecom For Dummies.* Hoboken, NJ: John Wiley and Sons, Inc, 2006.

However, telephone companies have been reducing the number of technicians they need in recent years, and competition for these positions is especially heavy.

Information on job openings in this field may be available through the offices of the state employment service and through classified advertisements in newspapers. Because many communications equipment technicians are members of unions such as the Communications Workers of America (CWA) and the International Brotherhood of Electrical Workers (IBEW), job seekers can contact their local offices for job leads and assistance, or visit the CWA's and the IBEW's Web sites. The Personal Communications Industry Association also offers free job listings on its Wireless Jobnet online. Graduates of technical programs may be able to find out about openings at local companies through the school's career services office or through contacts with teachers and administrators.

ADVANCEMENT

The advancement possibilities for communications equipment technicians depend on the area of the telecommunications industry in which they work. Because of changes in equipment and technology, workers who hope to advance will need to have received recent training or update their skills through additional training. This training may be offered through employers or can be obtained through technical institutes or telecommunications associations.

Advancement opportunities in telephone companies may be limited because of the fact that many telephone companies are reducing their workforces and will have less need for certain types of workers in the future. This will result in fewer positions to move into and increased competition for more advanced positions. However, some workers may be able to advance to supervisory or administrative positions.

Many workers can advance through education resulting in an associate's or bachelor's degree. Workers who have completed two- or four-year programs in electrical or telecommunications engineering programs have the best opportunity to advance and can become engineering assistants, engineers, or telecommunications specialists.

EARNINGS

Earnings vary among communications equipment workers depending on their area of specialization, the size of their employer, and their location. The U.S. Department of Labor reports the following median annual earnings for telecommunication equipment install-ers and repairers by employer in 2006: satellite communications, $55,290; wired telecommunications carriers, $53,840; wireless telecommunications carriers (except satellite), $49,050; and cable and other program distribution, $44,180. Salaries for all telecom-munication equipment installers and repairers ranged from less than $31,110 to $68,310 or more.

Most workers in this group who are employed by telephone com-panies are union members, and their earnings are set by contracts between the union and the company. Many currently employed com-munications equipment technicians have several years of experience and are at the higher end of the pay scale. Most workers in this field receive extra pay for hours worked at night, on weekends, or over 40 hours a week. Benefits vary but generally include paid vacations, paid holidays, sick leaves, and health insurance. In addition, some companies offer pension and retirement plans.

WORK ENVIRONMENT

Communications equipment technicians usually work 40 hours a week. Some work shifts at night, on weekends, and on holidays because telecommunications systems must give uninterrupted ser-vice and trouble can occur at any time.

Central telephone offices are clean, well lighted, and well venti-lated. Communications equipment technicians may also be working on site, which may require some crawling around on office floors and some bending. Even if these workers are running cables, they aren't likely to be doing much heavy lifting; machinery assists them in some of the more strenuous work. These workers may work alone, or they may be supervising the work of others. Some communica-tions equipment technicians also work directly with clients.

The work can be stressful, as technicians are often expected to work quickly to remedy urgent problems with communication equip-ment. Some technicians who work for large companies with clients nationwide must also travel as part of their jobs.

OUTLOOK

The U.S. Department of Labor predicts that the overall employment rate for communications equipment technicians will remain about the same through 2016. Job availability will depend on the technician's area of specialization. For example, technicians working as central office and PBX installers should find numerous job opportunities, in part because growing use of the Internet places new demands on communications networks. On the other hand, pre-wired buildings and extremely reliable equipment will translate into less need for maintenance and repair, which will limit employment opportunities for some installers and repairers. New technology relies on transmission through telecommunications networks rather than central-office switching equipment. There are far fewer mechanical devices that break, wear out, and need to be periodically cleaned and lubricated. These networks contain self-diagnosing features that detect problems and, in some cases, route operations around a trouble spot until repairs can be made. When problems occur, it is usually easier to replace parts rather than repair them. Competition for existing positions will be keen, and workers with the best qualifications stand the best chance of obtaining available jobs.

FOR MORE INFORMATION

To learn about issues affecting jobs in telecommunications, contact the following organizations:
Communications Workers of America (CWA)
501 Third Street, NW
Washington, DC 20001-2797
Tel: 202-434-1100
http://www.cwa-union.org

International Brotherhood of Electrical Workers (IBEW)
900 Seventh Street, NW
Washington, DC 20001-3886
Tel: 202-833-7000
http://www.ibew.org

For information on certification, contact
International Association for Radio, Telecommunications and
   Electromagnetics
840 Queen Street
New Bern, NC 28560-4856
Tel: 800-896-2783
http://www.narte.org

For information on educational programs and job opportunities in wireless technology (cellular, PCS, and satellite), contact
Personal Communications Industry Association
901 North Washington Street, Suite 600
Alexandria VA 22314-1535

Tel: 800-759-0300
http://www.pcia.com

For information on careers, educational programs, educational seminars, distance learning, and certification, contact
Society of Cable Telecommunications Engineers
140 Philips Road
Exton, PA 19341-1318
Tel: 800-542-5040
Email: scte@scte.org
http://www.scte.org

For information on certification, contact
Telecommunications Industry Association
2500 Wilson Boulevard, Suite 300
Arlington, VA 22201-3834
Tel: 703-907-7700
http://www.tiaonline.org

For information about conferences, special programs, and membership, contact
Women in Cable and Telecommunications
14555 Avion Parkway, Suite 250
Chantilly, VA 20151-1117
Tel: 703-234-9810
http://www.wict.org

Computer Engineers

OVERVIEW

Computer engineers may specialize in either software—the programs used to run computers—or hardware—the physical parts of a computer, or work in both specialties. Software engineers are responsible for customizing existing software programs to meet the needs and desires of a particular business or industry. Hardware engineers design, build, and test computer hardware and computer systems. Most computer engineers have a degree in computer science, engineering, or equivalent computer background and knowledge. There are about 936,000 computer engineers employed in the United States. Fewer than 35,000 computer engineers are employed in the telecommunications industry.

HISTORY

What started as a specialty of electrical engineering has developed into a career field of its own. Today, many individuals interested in a career in one of the computer industry's most promising sectors turn to computer engineering. Computer engineers improve, repair, and implement changes needed to keep up with the demand for faster and stronger computers and complex software programs. Some specialize in the design of the hardware: computer or peripheral parts such as memory chips, motherboards, or microprocessors. Others specialize in creating and organizing information systems for businesses and the government.

Computer engineers play a key role in the telecommunications industry—helping to design, build, and troubleshoot a wide variety of equipment, devices, and products. The Society of Cable Tele-communications Engineers was founded in 1969 to represent the professional interests of engineers (including those who specialize in computer engineering).

THE JOB

There are two main types of computer engineers: *software engineers* and *hardware engineers.*

Software engineers define and analyze specific problems, and help develop computer software applications that effectively solve them. They fall into two basic categories: *systems software engineers* and *applications software engineers.*

Systems software engineers build and maintain entire computer systems for a telecommunications company. For example, a company may need a new order processing system that tracks customer requests, the movements and work of technicians, and fulfills other specifications. Systems software engineers suggest ways to coordinate all these utilities and design the computer systems that will allow this information to be gathered and be seamlessly displayed to customer service representatives.

Applications software engineers design, create, and modify general computer applications software and specialized utility programs. They might help create installation software that will be used by customers when they purchase a new cell phone or sign up for broadband Internet service. Some applications software engineers might develop the software that provides ringtones, games, and other applications on cell phones or other handheld devices. Others might develop a software security program that protects customers' credit card and other private information in company databases.

Computer hardware engineers work with the physical parts of computers, such as CPUs (computer processing units), motherboards, chipsets, video cards, cooling units, disk drives, storage devices, processors, network cards, and all the components that connect them, down to wires, nuts, and bolts. They are also responsible for all peripheral devices such as printers, scanners, keyboards, modems, and monitors, digital cameras, external storage, and speaker systems, among other devices. They also help design and build cell phones, wired telephones, cable box technology, high-definition receivers, and large computer and electronic infrastructure and systems used by the telecommunications industry. Hardware engineers also design parts and create prototypes using CAD/CAM technology. For example, a hardware engineer employed by Verizon could use this technology to help re-engineer video cards for a new cell phone model to improve picture quality and speed.

Both software and hardware engineers must be extremely detail oriented. Software engineers must account for every bit of information accrued by a programming command. Hardware components must often be designed or revised to certain specifications, and may change as the project proceeds. Computer engineers often work with other engineers, scientists, and company executives in order to complete a project.

Computer engineers are usually responsible for a significant amount of technical writing, including project proposals, progress reports, and user manuals. They are required to meet regularly with clients and managers to keep project goals clear and learn about any changes as quickly as possible.

REQUIREMENTS

High School

A bachelor's or advanced degree in computer science or engineering is required for most computer engineers. Thus, to prepare for college studies while in high school, take as many computer, math, and science courses as possible; they provide fundamental math and computer knowledge and teach analytical thinking skills. Classes that rely on schematic drawing and flowcharts are also very valuable. English and speech courses will help you improve your communication skills, which are very important for computer engineers.

Postsecondary Training

Computer engineers need at least a bachelor's degree in computer engineering, hardware engineering, software engineering, computer science, or electrical engineering. Employment in research laboratories or academic institutions might require a master's or Ph.D. in computer science or engineering. For a list of accredited four-year computer engineering programs, contact the Accreditation Board for Engineering and Technology (http://www.abet.org).

The intense and diverse course study and the significant time required to obtain a postsecondary degree in computer engineering requires a variety of skills and abilities. In addition to natural ability, you should be hard working and determined to succeed. If you plan to work in a specific field, such as telecommunications, you should receive some formal training in that particular discipline.

Certification or Licensing

Not all computer professionals are certified. The deciding factor seems to be whether certification is required by their employer. Many companies offer tuition reimbursement, or incentives, to those who earn certification. Certification is available in a variety of specialties. The Institute for Certification of Computing Professionals offers the associate computing professional designation for those new to the field and the certified computing professional designation for those with at least 48 months of full-time professional level work in computer-based information systems. Additionally, the Society of Cable Telecommunications Engineers and the International Association for Radio, Telecommunications and Electromagnetics offer certification for engineers employed in the telecommunications industry. Certification is considered by many to be a measure of industry knowledge as well as leverage when negotiating salary.

Other Requirements

Computer engineers need a broad knowledge of and experience with computer systems, software, and technologies. You need strong problem-solving and analysis skills and good interpersonal skills. You must also be detail oriented and work well under pressure. Patience, self-motivation, and flexibility are important. Often, a number of projects are worked on simultaneously, so the ability to multitask is important. Because of rapid technological advances in the computer field, continuing education is a necessity.

EXPLORING

Try to spend a day with a working computer engineer or technician in order to experience first-hand what their job is like. School guidance counselors can help you arrange such a visit. You can also talk to your high school computer teacher for more information.

In general, you should be intent on learning as much as possible about computers and computer software and hardware. You should learn about new developments by reading trade magazines and talking to other computer users. You also can join computer clubs and surf the Internet for information about working in this field.

If you are interested in working in telecommunications, you should learn as much as you can about the industry as possible. Read industry publications such as *IEEE Wireless Communication Magazine* (http://www.comsoc.org/pubs/pcm) and *Communications Technology* (http://www.cable360.net/ct) and visit the Web sites of professional associations (see For More Information).

EMPLOYERS

Approximately 936,000 computer engineers are employed in the United States. About 857,000 computer engineers work with computer software; an additional 79,000 work with computer hardware. Fewer than 35,000 computer engineers are employed in the telecommunications industry. Computer engineers are employed by wired and wireless telecommunications carriers, cable and other program distributors, and manufacturing companies that serve the telecommunications industry. Major telecommunications companies include Qualcomm, AT&T, Verizon, Motorola, Nokia, Sony, Comcast Cable Communications, Time Warner Cable, Cox Communications, DirecTV, and Dish Network Services.

STARTING OUT

As a technical, vocational, or university student of computer engineering, you should work closely with your school's career services office, as many professionals find their first position through on-campus recruiting. Career service office staff are well trained to provide tips on resume writing, interviewing techniques, and locating job leads.

Individuals not working with a school career services office can check the classified ads for job openings. They also can work with a local employment agency that places computer professionals in appropriate jobs. Many openings in the computer industry are publicized by word of mouth, so you should stay in touch with working computer professionals to learn who is hiring. In addition, these people may be willing to refer you directly to the person in charge of recruiting.

Computer engineers who are interested in working for telecommunications companies should contact these companies directly for information on employment opportunities. Professional associations—such as the Society of Cable Telecommunications Engineers and the International Association for Radio, Telecommunications and Electromagnetics—also offer job listings at their Web sites.

ADVANCEMENT

Computer engineers who demonstrate leadership qualities and thorough technical know-how may become *project team leaders* who are responsible for full-scale software and hardware development projects. Project team leaders oversee the work of technicians and engineers. They determine the overall parameters of a project, calculate time schedules and financial budgets, divide the project into smaller tasks, and assign these tasks to engineers. Overall, they do both managerial and technical work.

Computer engineers with experience as project team leaders may be promoted to a position as *computer manager,* running a large research and development department. Managers oversee software projects with a more encompassing perspective; they help choose projects to be undertaken, select project team leaders and engineering teams, and assign individual projects. In some cases, they may be required to travel, solicit new business, and contribute to the general marketing strategy of the company.

Many computer professionals find that their interests change over time. As long as individuals are well qualified and keep up to date with the latest technology, they are usually able to find positions in other areas of the computer industry.

EARNINGS

Starting salary offers in 2007 for bachelor's degree candidates in computer engineering averaged $56,201, according to the National Association of Colleges and Employers. Those with a master's degree averaged $60,000, and new graduates with a Ph.D. averaged $92,500.

The U.S. Department of Labor reports that computer engineers employed in the telecommunications industry earned the following mean salary by specialty in 2006: software-applications, $82,450; software-systems software, $84,170; and hardware, $83,250.

Salaries for all computer software engineers ranged from less than $49,000 to $125,000 or more. Hardware engineers employed in all industries earned salaries that ranged from less than $53,000 to more than $135,000.

When computer engineers are promoted to project team leader or computer manager, they can earn even more. Computer engineers generally earn more in geographical areas where there are clusters of computer companies, such as the Silicon Valley in northern California.

Most computer engineers work for companies that offer extensive benefits, including health insurance, sick leave, and paid vacation. In some smaller computer companies, however, benefits may be limited.

WORK ENVIRONMENT

Computer engineers usually work in comfortable office environments. Overall, they usually work 40-hour weeks, but this depends on the nature of the employer and expertise of the engineer. In consulting firms, for example, it is typical for engineers to work long hours and frequently travel to out-of-town assignments.

Computer engineers generally receive an assignment and a time frame within which to accomplish it; daily work details are often left up to the individuals. Some engineers work relatively lightly at the beginning of a project, but work a lot of overtime at the end in order to catch up. Most engineers are not compensated for overtime. Computer engineering can be stressful, especially when engineers must work to meet deadlines. Working with programming languages and intense details, for example, is often frustrating. Therefore, computer engineers should be patient, enjoy problem-solving challenges, and work well under pressure.

OUTLOOK

Employment for computer software engineers employed in telecommunications is expected to grow by 9 percent through 2016—or about as fast as the average for all occupations. Telecommunications companies will continue to implement new and innovative technology to remain competitive, and they will need software engineers to do this. Software engineers will also be needed to handle the ever-growing capabilities of computer networks, e-commerce, and wireless technologies, as well as the security features needed to protect such systems from outside attacks. Overall, the field of software engineering is expected to be one of the fastest growing occupations through 2016. Demands made on computers increase every day and from all industries. Rapid growth in the computer systems design and related industries will account for much of this growth.

Employment in hardware engineering will grow more slowly than the average for all occupations through 2016, according to the U.S. Department of Labor. Foreign competition and increased productivity at U.S. companies will limit opportunities for hardware engineers. Opportunities will be best for hardware engineers who are employed in computer systems design and related services.

FOR MORE INFORMATION

For information on internships, student membership, and the student magazine Crossroads, *contact*
Association for Computing Machinery
2 Penn Plaza Suite 701
New York, NY 10121-0701

Tel: 212-869-7440
http://www.acm.org

For certification information, contact
Institute for Certification of Computing Professionals
2350 East Devon Avenue, Suite 115
Des Plaines, IL 60018-4610
Tel: 800-843-8227
Email: office@iccp.org
http://www.iccp.org

For information on scholarships, student membership, and the student newsletter, looking.forward, *contact*
IEEE Computer Society
1828 L Street, NW, Suite 1202
Washington, DC 20036-5104
Tel: 202-371-0101
http://www.computer.org

For information on certification, contact
International Association for Radio, Telecommunications and Electromagnetics
840 Queen Street
New Bern, NC 28560-4856
Tel: 800-896-2783
http://www.narte.org

For information on careers, educational programs, educational seminars, distance learning, and certification, contact
Society of Cable Telecommunications Engineers
140 Philips Road
Exton, PA 19341-1318
Tel: 800-542-5040
Email: scte@scte.org
http://www.scte.org

Computer Support Specialists

OVERVIEW

Computer support specialists investigate and resolve technical problems for customers in the telecommunications industry. They help customers troubleshoot a variety of products including wired and wireless phones, personal digital assistants, cable and high-definition receivers, computer software, and other equipment. They listen to customer complaints, walk customers through possible solutions, and write technical reports based on their work. Computer support specialists must be very knowledgeable about the products with which they work and be able to communicate effectively with users from different technical backgrounds. They must be patient and professional with frustrated users and be able to perform well under stress. Computer support is similar to solving mysteries, so support specialists should enjoy the challenge of problem solving and have strong analytical skills. There are approximately 13,000 computer support specialists employed in the telecommunications industry in the United States.

HISTORY

Computer support has been around since the development of the first telecommunications technology for the simple reason that, like all machines, phones and other technology experience problems at one time or another.

As more and more companies offer telecommunications products, smart executives have realized that strong computer support departments are one of the keys to success in the field. Customers need to have confidence that their problems will be addressed competently and efficiently. A company uses its reputation and the availability of its computer support department to differentiate its products and services from those of other companies, even though the tangible products like basic cable service, for example, may actually be nearly identical.

The goal of any company is to offer a product or service that requires no computer support, so that the computer support department has minimal work to complete. Given the speed of development, however, computer support departments will still have to provide, at least, a moderate level of support for their respective company's products and services. Until the time arrives when users of computers are able to resolve all questions and problems without the assistance of a human computer support specialist, there will be a strong demand for these critical telecommunication professionals.

THE JOB

In the telecommunications industry, computer support can generally be broken up into two distinct areas, although these distinctions vary greatly with the nature, size, and scope of the company. The two most prevalent areas are user support and technical support. Most computer support specialists perform some combination of the tasks explained below.

The jobs of computer support specialists vary according to whom they assist and what they fix. Some specialists help private users exclusively; others are on call to a major corporate buyer. Some specialists work with telecommunications software, and others work with hardware. *User support specialists,* also known as *help desk specialists,* work directly with customers, or users, who call, email, or communicate in real-time online when they experience problems. The support specialist listens carefully to the user's explanation of the precise nature of the problem (i.e., cell phone won't turn on, no cable signal, heavy static on a telephone line, the software the customer installed to set up an Internet connection will not work, etc.), and tries to suggest solutions. Some companies have developed complex software that allows the support specialist to enter a description of the problem and wait for the computer to provide suggestions about what the user should do to resolve the problem.

The initial goal is to isolate the source of the problem. If user error is the culprit, the user support specialist explains procedures related to the program in question. If the problem seems to lie in the hardware or software, the specialist asks the user to enter certain commands in order to see if the device makes the appropriate response. If it does not, the support specialist is closer to isolating the cause of the problem. The support specialist consults supervisors, programmers, and others in order to outline the cause of the service interruption and suggest possible solutions.

Technical support specialists employed in the information systems departments of telecommunications companies are mainly involved with solving in-house computer problems whose cause has been determined to lie in the computer system's operating system, hardware, or software. They make exhaustive use of resources, such as colleagues or books, and try to solve the problem through a variety of methods, including program modifications and the replacement of certain hardware or software. Technical support specialists also oversee the daily operations of the various computer systems in the company. Sometimes they compare the system's work capacity to the actual daily workload in order to determine if upgrades are needed. In addition, they might help out other computer professionals in the company with modifying commercial software for their company's particular needs.

All computer support work must be well-documented. Support specialists write detailed technical reports on every problem they work on. They try to tie together different problems on the same software or hardware, so programmers or engineers can make adjustments that address all of the issues. Record keeping is crucial because designers, programmers, and engineers use technical support reports to revise current products and improve future ones. Some support specialists help write training manuals. They are often required to read trade magazines and company newsletters in order to keep up to date on their products and the field in general.

REQUIREMENTS

High School
A high school diploma is a minimum requirement for computer support specialists. Any technical courses you can take, such as computer science and electronics, can help you develop the logical and analytical thinking skills necessary to be successful in this field. Courses in math and science are also valuable for this reason. Since computer support specialists have to deal with both computer professionals on the one hand and customers who may not know anything about technology, on the other, you should take English and speech classes to improve your verbal and written communications skills.

Postsecondary Training

Individuals interested in pursuing a job in this field should first determine what area of computer support appeals to them the most and then honestly assess their level of experience and knowledge. Large corporations often prefer to hire people with an associate's degree and some experience. They may also be impressed with commercial certification in a computer field, such as networking. However, if they are hiring from within the company, they will probably weigh experience more heavily than education when making a final decision.

Employed individuals looking for a career change may want to commit themselves to a program of self-study in order to be qualified for computer support positions. Many computer professionals learn a lot of what they know by playing around with technology, reading trade magazines, and talking with colleagues. Self-taught individuals should learn how to effectively demonstrate their knowledge and proficiency on the job or during an interview. Besides self-training, employed individuals should investigate tuition reimbursement programs offered by their company.

There are many computer technology programs that lead to an associate's degree. A specialization in personal computer support and administration is certainly applicable to work in computer support. Most computer professionals eventually need to go back to school to earn a bachelor's degree in order to keep themselves competitive in the job market and prepare themselves for promotion to other computer fields.

Certification or Licensing

Computer associations, such as HDI and CompTIA: The Computing Technology Industry Association, offer certification for support specialists who primarily are employed in the computer industry. These certifications would be useful to technical support specialists who are employed in the information systems departments of their companies and solve in-house issues. However, they are not that useful to user support specialists employed in the telecommunications industry.

To become certified, you will need to pass a written test and in some cases may need a certain amount of work experience. Although going through the certification process is voluntary, becoming certified will most likely be to your advantage. It will show your commitment to the profession as well as demonstrate your level of expertise. In addition, certification may qualify you for certain jobs and lead to new employment opportunities.

A senior support specialist at a Qwest network reliability center talks on the phone to troubleshoot a problem. *(Jack Dempsey, Associated Press)*

Other Requirements

To be a successful computer support specialist, you should be patient, enjoy challenges of problem solving, and think logically. You should work well under stress and demonstrate effective communication skills. Since you will be working in a field that changes rapidly, you should be naturally curious and enthusiastic about learning new technologies as they are developed.

EXPLORING

If you are interested in becoming a computer support specialist, you should try to organize a career day with a computer support specialist who is employed in the telecommunications industry.

If you are interested in working in telecommunications, ask to help your parents with software installations or other set-ups for new phones, cable boxes, or Internet service. Visit the computer support sections at telecommunication company Web sites to get an idea of how computer support is handled. In addition, if you experience problems with your own phone or cable service, you should call computer support, paying careful attention to how the support specialist handles the call and ask as many questions as the specialist has time to answer.

EMPLOYERS

Computer support specialists work for telecommunications companies including Qualcomm, AT&T, Motorola, Verizon, Nokia, Sony, Comcast Cable Communications, Time Warner Cable, Cox Communications, DirecTV, and Dish Network Services. Approximately 13,000 computer support specialists are employed in the telecommunications industry in the United States.

Computer support specialists also work for computer hardware and software companies, as well as in the information systems departments of large corporations and government agencies.

STARTING OUT

Most computer support positions are considered entry-level. Individuals interested in obtaining a job in this field should scan the classified ads for openings at local companies and may want to work with an employment agency for help finding out about opportunities.

One of the best ways to learn about employment opportunities in the telecommunications industry is to visit the Web sites of major companies in the field. Most feature an extensive overview of career opportunities in the field. Some even allow you to post your resume.

If students of computer technology are seeking a position in computer support, they should work closely with their school's career services office. Many employers inform career services offices at nearby schools of openings before ads are run in the newspaper. In addition, career services office staffs are generally very helpful with resume writing assistance and interviewing techniques.

If an employee wants to make a career change into computer support, he or she should contact the human resources department of the company or speak directly with appropriate management.

ADVANCEMENT

Computer support specialists who demonstrate leadership skills and a strong aptitude for the work may be promoted to supervisory positions within computer support departments. Supervisors are responsible for the more complicated problems that arise, as well as for some administrative duties such as scheduling, interviewing, and job assignments.

There are limited opportunities for computer support specialists to be promoted into managerial positions. Job advancement into managerial positions requires additional education in business but would probably also depend on the individual's advanced computer knowledge.

EARNINGS

Median annual earnings for computer support specialists employed in the telecommunications industry were $46,090 in 2006, according to the U.S. Department of Labor. Salaries for computer support specialists employed in all industries ranged from less than $25,290 to $68,540 or more annually. Those who have more education, responsibility, and expertise have the potential to earn much more.

Most computer support specialists work for companies that offer a full range of benefits, including health insurance, paid vacation, and sick leave. Smaller service or start-up companies may hire support specialists on a contractual basis.

WORK ENVIRONMENT

Computer support specialists work in comfortable business environments. They generally work regular, 40-hour weeks. For certain products, however, they may be asked to work evenings or weekends or at least be on call during those times in case of emergencies.

Computer support work can be stressful, since specialists often deal with frustrated users who may be difficult to work with. Communication problems with people who are less technically qualified may also be a source of frustration. Patience and understanding are essential for handling these problems.

Computer support specialists are expected to work quickly and efficiently and be able to perform under pressure. The ability to do this requires thorough technical expertise and keen analytical ability.

OUTLOOK

The U.S. Department of Labor predicts that employment for computer support specialists (including those employed in the telecommunications industry) will grow about as fast as the average for all occupations through 2016. Each time a new product is released on the market or another system is installed, there will be problems, whether from user error or technical difficulty. Therefore, there will always be a need for computer support specialists to solve the problems. Since technology changes so rapidly, it is very important for these professionals to keep up to date on advances. They should read trade magazines, surf the Internet, and talk with colleagues in order to know what is happening in the field.

FOR MORE INFORMATION

To learn more about membership and career training seminars, contact

Association of Computer Support Specialists
333 Mamaroneck Avenue, #129
White Plains, NY 10605-1440
http://www.acss.org

For salary surveys and other information, contact
Association of Support Professionals
122 Barnard Avenue
Watertown, MA 02472-3414
Tel: 617-924-3944
http://www.asponline.com

For information on certification, contact
CompTIA: The Computing Technology Industry Association
1815 South Meyers Road, Suite 300
Oakbrook Terrace, IL 60181-5228
Tel: 630-678-8300
http://www.comptia.org

For job postings, links to wireless industry recruiters, industry news, and training information, visit the CTIA Web site:
CTIA-The Wireless Association
1400 16th Street, NW, Suite 600
Washington, DC 20036-2225
Tel: 202-785-0081
http://www.ctia.org

For more information on this organization's training courses and certification, contact
HDI
102 South Tejon, Suite 1200
Colorado Springs, CO 80903-2231
Tel: 800-248-5667
Email: support@thinkhdi.com
http://www.thinkhdi.com

For information on careers and the cable industry, contact
National Cable & Telecommunications Association
25 Massachusetts Avenue, NW, Suite 100
Washington, DC 20001-1434

Tel: 202-222-2300
http://www.ncta.com

For information on educational programs and job opportunities in wireless technology (cellular, PCS, and satellite), contact
Personal Communications Industry Association
901 North Washington Street, Suite 600
Alexandria VA 22314-1535
Tel: 800-759-0300
http://www.pcia.com

For information about telecommunications, contact
Telecommunications Industry Association
2500 Wilson Boulevard, Suite 300
Arlington, VA 22201-3834
Tel: 703-907-7700
http://www.tiaonline.org

Customer Service Representatives

OVERVIEW

Customer service representatives, sometimes called *customer care representatives,* work with customers of one or many companies, assist with customer problems, or answer questions. Customer service representatives work in many different industries, including telecommunications, to provide "frontline" customer service in a variety of businesses. Most customer service representatives work in an office setting though some may work in the "field" to better meet customer needs. There are approximately 137,000 customer service representatives employed in the telecommunications industry in the United States.

HISTORY

Customer service has been a part of business for many years; however, the formal title of customer service representative is relatively new. In 1988, the International Customer Service Association established Customer Service Week to recognize and promote customer service.

As the world moves toward a more global and competitive economic market, customer service, along with quality control, has taken a front seat in the business world. Serving customers and serving them well is more important now than ever before.

Customer service is about communication, so the progress in customer service can be tied closely to the progress in the telecommunications industry. When Alexander Graham Bell invented the telephone in 1876, he probably did not envision the customer service lines, automated response messages, toll-free phone numbers, and computer technology that now help customer service representatives do their jobs.

The increased use of the Internet has helped companies serve and communicate with their customers in another way. From the simple email complaint form to online help files, telecommunications companies, as well as those in other industries, are using the Internet to provide better customer service. Some companies even have online chat capabilities to communicate with their customers instantaneously on the Web.

THE JOB

Julia Cox is a customer service representative for Affina. Affina is a call center that handles customer service for a variety of companies, including those in the telecommunications industry. Cox works with each of Affina's clients and the call center operators to ensure that each call-in receives top customer service.

Customer service representatives often handle complaints and problems, and Cox finds that to be the case at the call center as well. While the operators who report to her provide customer service to those on the phone, Cox must oversee that customer service while also keeping in mind the customer service for her client, whatever business they may be in.

"I make sure that the clients get regular reports of the customer service calls and check to see if there are any recurring problems," says Cox.

One of the ways Cox observes if customer service is not being handled effectively is by monitoring the actual time spent on each phone call. If an operator spends a lot of time on a call, there is most likely a problem.

"Our customers are billed per minute," says Cox. "So we want to make sure their customer service is being handled well and efficiently."

Affina's call center in Columbus, Indiana, handles dozens of toll-free lines. While some calls are likely to be focused on complaints or questions, some are easier to handle. Cox and her staff handle calls from people simply wanting to order literature, brochures, or to find their nearest dealer location.

Customer service representatives work in a variety of fields and businesses, but one thing is common—the customer. All businesses depend on their customers to keep them in business, so customer service, whether handled internally or outsourced to a call center like Affina, is extremely important.

Some customer service representatives, like Cox, do most of their work on the telephone. Others may represent companies in the field, where the customer is actually using the product or service. Still other customer service representatives may specialize in Internet service, assisting customers over the World Wide Web via email or online chats.

Affina's call center is available to their clients 24 hours a day, seven days a week, so Cox and her staff must keep around-the-clock shifts. Not all customer service representatives work a varied schedule; many work a traditional daytime shift. However, customers have problems, complaints, and questions 24 hours a day, so many companies do staff their customer service positions for a longer number of hours, especially to accommodate customers during evenings and weekends.

REQUIREMENTS

High School

A high school diploma is required for most customer service representative positions. High school courses that emphasize communication, such as English and speech, will help you learn to communicate clearly. Any courses that require collaboration with others will also help to teach diplomacy and tact—two important aspects of customer service. Business courses will help you get a good overview of the business world, one that is dependent on customers and customer service. Computer skills are also very important.

Postsecondary Training

While a college degree is not necessary to become a customer service representative, certain areas of postsecondary training are helpful. Courses in business and organizational leadership will help to give you a better feel for the business world. Just as in high school, communications classes are helpful in learning to effectively talk with and meet the needs of other people.

These courses can be taken during a college curriculum or may be offered at a variety of customer service workshops or classes. Julia Cox is working as a customer service representative while she earns her business degree from a local college. Along with her college work, she has taken advantage of seminars and workshops to improve her customer service skills.

Bachelor's degrees in business and communications are increasingly required for managerial positions.

Customer service representatives in a call-center assist customers. *(Peter M. Fisher, Corbis)*

Certification or Licensing
Although it is not a requirement, a customer service representative can become certified. The International Customer Service Association offers certification to customer service professionals. Contact the association for more information.

Other Requirements
"The best and the worst parts of being a customer service representative are the people," Julia Cox says. Customer service representatives should have the ability to maintain a pleasant attitude at all times, even while serving angry or demanding customers.

A successful customer service representative will most likely have an outgoing personality and enjoy working with people and assisting them with their questions and problems.

Because many customer service representatives work in offices and on the telephone, people with physical disabilities may find this career to be both accessible and enjoyable.

EXPLORING

Julia Cox first discovered her love for customer service while working in retail at a local department store. Explore your ability for customer service by getting a job that deals with the public on a day-to-day basis. Talk with people who work with customers and customer service every day; find out what they like and dislike about their jobs.

There are other ways that you can prepare for a career in this field while you are still in school. Join your school's business club to get a feel for what goes on in the business world today. Doing volunteer work for a local charity or homeless shelter can help you decide if serving others is something that you'd enjoy doing as a career.

Evaluate the customer service at the businesses you visit. What makes that salesperson at The Gap better than the operator you talked with last week? Volunteer to answer phones at an agency in your town or city. Most receptionists in small companies and agencies are called on to provide customer service to callers. Try a nonprofit organization. They will welcome the help, and you will get a firsthand look at customer service.

EMPLOYERS

Customer service representatives are hired at all types of companies in a variety of areas. Industries that employ large numbers of customer service representatives include information, particularly the telecommunications industry; administrative and support services; retail trade establishments such as general merchandise stores and food and beverage stores; manufacturing, such as printing and related support activities; and wholesale trade. Because all businesses rely on customers, customer service is generally a high priority for those businesses. Some companies, like call centers, may employ a large number of customer service representatives to serve a multitude of clients, while small businesses may simply have one or two people who are responsible for customer service.

Approximately 30 percent of customer service representatives are employed in four states (California, Texas, Florida, and New York), but opportunities are available throughout the United States. In the United States, approximately 137,000 workers are employed as customer service representatives in the telecommunications industry. Large telecommunications companies include Qualcomm, AT&T, Motorola, Verizon, Nokia, Sony, Motorola, Comcast Cable Communications, Time Warner Cable, Cox Communications, DirecTV, and Dish Network Services.

STARTING OUT

You can become a customer service representative as an entry-level applicant, although some customer service representatives have first served in other areas of a company. This company experience may provide customer service representatives with more knowledge and experience to answer customer questions. A college degree is not required, but any postsecondary training will increase your ability to find a job in customer service.

Ads for customer service job openings are readily available in newspapers and on Internet job search sites. You should also visit the Web sites of telecommunications companies for job listings. With some experience and a positive attitude, it is possible to move into the position of customer service representative from another job within the company. Julia Cox started out at Affina as an operator and quickly moved into a customer service capacity.

ADVANCEMENT

Customer service experience is valuable in any business career path. Julia Cox hopes to combine her customer service experience with a business degree and move to the human resources area of her company.

It is also possible to advance to management or marketing jobs after working as a customer service representative. Businesses and their customers are inseparable, so most business professionals are experts at customer relations.

EARNINGS

Earnings vary based on location, level of experience, and size and type of employer. The U.S. Department of Labor reports the median annual income for customer service representatives employed by telecommunications companies as $32,490 in 2006. Salaries for all customer service representatives ranged from less than $18,110 to more than $45,990.

Other benefits vary widely according to the size and type of company in which representatives are employed. Benefits may include medical, dental, vision, and life insurance, 401(k) plans, or bonus incentives. Full-time customer service representatives can expect to receive vacation and sick pay, while part-time workers may not be offered these benefits.

WORK ENVIRONMENT

Customer service representatives work primarily indoors, although some may work in the field where the customers are using the product

U.S. Cable Industry Statistics, 2007

U.S. Television Households:	111,600,000
Basic Cable Customers:	65,600,000
Premium Cable Units:	50,600,000
2007 Annual Cable Revenue:	$74.7 billion
Cable Systems:	7,090
National Cable Networks:	531

Source: National Cable & Telecommunications Association

or service. They usually work in a supervised setting and report to a manager. They may spend many hours on the telephone, answering mail, or handling Internet communication. Many of the work hours involve little physical activity.

While most customer service representatives generally work a 40-hour workweek, others work a variety of shifts. Many businesses want customer service hours to coincide with the times that their customers are available to call or contact the business. For many companies, these times are in the evenings and on the weekends, so some customer service representatives work a varied shift and odd hours.

OUTLOOK

The U.S. Department of Labor predicts that employment for all customer service representatives (including those employed in the telecommunications industry) will grow much faster than the average for all occupations through 2016. This is a large field of workers and many replacement workers are needed each year as customer service reps leave this job for other positions, retire, or leave for other reasons. In addition, the Internet and e-commerce should increase the need for customer service representatives who will be needed to help customers navigate Web sites, answer questions over the phone, and respond to emails.

For customer service representatives with specific knowledge of a product or business, the outlook is very good, as quick, efficient customer service is valuable in any business. Additional training and education and proficiency in a foreign language will also make finding a job as a customer service representative an easier task.

FOR MORE INFORMATION

For information on jobs, training, workshops, and salaries, contact
Customer Care Institute
17 Dean Overlook, NW
Atlanta, GA 30318-1663
Tel: 404-352-9291
Email: info@customercare.com
http://www.customercare.com

For information about the customer service industry, contact
HDI
102 South Tejon, Suite 1200
Colorado Springs, CO 80903-2242
Tel: 800-248-5667
Email: support@thinkhdi.com
http://www.thinkhdi.com

For information on international customer service careers and certification, contact
International Customer Service Association
401 North Michigan Avenue
Chicago, IL 60611-4255
Tel: 800-360-4272
Email: icsa@smithbucklin.com
http://www.icsa.com

For information on education and careers in telecommunications, contact
NACTEL, The National Coalition For Telecommunications Education and Learning
6021 South Syracuse Way, Suite 213
Greenwood Village, CO 80111-4747
http://www.nactel.org

Electrical and Electronics Engineers

OVERVIEW

Electrical engineers apply their knowledge of the sciences to working with equipment that produces and distributes electricity, such as generators, transmission lines, and transformers. This equipment is used in the telecommunications industry and other fields. They also design, develop, and manufacture electric motors, electrical machinery, and ignition systems for automobiles, aircraft, and other engines. *Electronics engineers* are more concerned with devices made up of electronic components such as integrated circuits and microprocessors. They design, develop, and manufacture products such as computers, telephones, satellite receivers, and radios. Electronics engineering is a subfield of electrical engineering, and both types of engineers are often referred to as electrical engineers. There are approximately 26,000 electrical and electronics engineers employed in the telecommunications industry in the United States.

HISTORY

Electrical and electronics engineering had their true beginnings in the 19th century. In 1800, Alexander Volta made a discovery that opened a door to the science of electricity—he found that electric current could be harnessed and made to flow. By the mid-1800s the basic rules of electricity were established, and the first practical applications appeared. At that time, Michael Faraday discovered the phenomenon of electromagnetic induction. Further discoveries followed. In 1837 Samuel Morse invented the telegraph; in 1876 Alexander Graham Bell invented the telephone; the incandescent lamp (the light bulb) was invented by Thomas Edison in 1878; and the first electric motor was invented by Nicholas Tesla in 1888 (Faraday had built a primitive model of one in 1821). These inventions required the further generation and harnessing of electricity, so efforts were concentrated on developing ways to produce more and more power and to create better equipment, such as motors and transformers.

Edison's invention led to a dependence on electricity for lighting our homes, work areas, and streets. He later created the phonograph and other electrical instruments, leading to the establishment of his General Electric Company. One of today's major telephone companies also had its beginnings during this time. Alexander Bell's invention led to the establishment of the Bell Telephone Company, which eventually became American Telephone and Telegraph (AT&T).

The roots of electronics, which is distinguished from the science of electricity by its focus on lower power generation, can also be found in the 19th century. In the late 1800s, current moving through space was observed for the first time; this was called the "Edison effect." In the early 20th century, devices (such as vacuum tubes, which are pieces of metal inside a glass bulb) were invented that could transmit weak electrical signals, leading to the potential transmission of electromagnetic waves for communication, or radio broadcast. The unreliability of vacuum tubes led to the invention of equipment that could pass electricity through solid materials; hence transistors came to be known as solid-state devices.

In the 1960s, transistors were being built on tiny bits of silicon, creating the microchip. The computer industry is a major beneficiary of the creation of these circuits, because vast amounts of information can be stored on just one tiny chip smaller than a dime.

The invention of microchips led to the development of microprocessors. Microprocessors are silicon chips on which the logic and arithmetic functions of a computer are placed. Microprocessors serve as miniature computers and are used in many types of products. The miniaturization of electronic components allowed scientists and engineers to make smaller, lighter computers that could perform the same, or additional, functions of larger computers. They also allowed for the development of many new products. At first they were used primarily in desktop calculators, video games, digital watches, telephones, and microwave ovens. Today, microprocessors are used in electronic controls of automobiles, personal computers, telecommunications systems, and many other products. As a leader in advanced technology, the electronics industry is one of the most important industries today.

Electrical and electronics engineers play an important role in the telecommunications industry—helping to design, build, and trouble-shoot a wide variety of equipment, devices, and products. The Society of Cable Telecommunications Engineers was formed in 1969 to represent the professional interests of engineers (including those who specialize in electrical and electronics engineering).

THE JOB

Because electrical and electronics engineering is such a diverse field, there are numerous divisions within which engineers work. In fact, the discipline reaches nearly every other field of applied science and technology. In general, electrical and electronics engineers use their knowledge of the sciences in the practical applications of electrical energy. They are involved in the invention, design, construction, and operation of electrical and electronic systems and devices of all kinds.

Electrical engineers in the telecommunications industry are concerned with how equipment is designed and maintained and how communications are transmitted via wire and airwaves. Some are involved in the design and construction of cell towers and other telecommunications infrastructure and the manufacture and maintenance of industrial machinery.

After electrical systems are put in place, *field service engineers* must act as the liaison between the manufacturer or distributor and the client. They ensure the correct installation, operation, and maintenance of systems and products for both industry and individuals.

Electronics engineers work with smaller-scale applications, such as how computers are wired, how cell phones work, or how circuits are used in an endless number of applications. They may test wired and wireless phones, cable and satellite receivers, personal digital assistants, and other electronics. Electronics engineers may specialize in just one part of a cell phone or other product, such as the antenna or power system for a cell phone.

Design and testing are only two of several categories in which electrical and electronics engineers may find their niche. Others include research and development and production. In addition, even within each category there are divisions of labor.

Researchers concern themselves mainly with issues that pertain to potential applications. They conduct tests and perform studies to evaluate fundamental problems involving such things as improving the battery power of telephones, extending the reach of cell phone networks via cutting-edge technology, or converting radio frequency cell phone signals to digital to improve transmission quality. Those who work in design and development adapt the researchers' findings to actual practical applications. They devise functioning devices and draw up plans for their efficient production, using computer-aided design and engineering (CAD/CAE) tools. For a typical product such as a cell phone, this phase usually takes up to 18 months to accomplish. For other products, particularly those that utilize developing technology, this phase can take as long as 10 years or more.

Production engineers have perhaps the most hands-on tasks in the field. They are responsible for the organization of the actual manufacture of whatever product is being made—whether it is a cell phone or a satellite dish. They take care of materials and machinery, schedule technicians and assembly workers, and make sure that standards are met and products are quality-controlled. These engineers must have access to the best tools for measurement, materials handling, and processing.

Whatever type of project an engineer works on, he or she is likely to have a certain amount of desk work. Writing status reports and communicating with clients and others who are working on the same project are examples of the paperwork that most engineers are responsible for.

REQUIREMENTS

High School
Electrical and electronics engineers must have a solid educational background, and the discipline requires a clear understanding of practical applications. To prepare for college, high school students should take classes in algebra, trigonometry, calculus, biology, physics, chemistry, computer science, word processing, English, and social studies. Business classes and computer skills are important as well. Students who are planning to pursue studies beyond a bachelor of science degree will also need to take a foreign language. It is recommended that students aim for honors-level courses.

Postsecondary Training
Numerous colleges and universities offer electrical, electronics, and computer engineering programs. Because the programs vary from one school to another, you should explore as many schools as possible to determine which program is most suited to your academic and personal interests and needs. Most engineering programs have strict admission requirements and require students to have excel-

lent academic records and top scores on national college-entrance examinations. Competition can be fierce for some programs, and high school students are encouraged to apply early.

Many students go on to receive a master of science degree in a specialization of their choice. This usually takes an additional two years of study beyond a bachelor's program. Some students pursue a master's degree immediately upon completion of a bachelor's degree. Other students, however, gain work experience first and then take graduate-level courses on a part-time basis while they are employed. A Ph.D. is also available. It generally requires four years of study and research beyond the bachelor's degree and is usually completed by people interested in research or teaching.

By the time you reach college, it is wise to be considering which type of engineering specialty you might be interested in. In addition to the core engineering curriculum (advanced mathematics, physical science, engineering science, mechanical drawing, computer applications), students will begin to choose from the following types of courses: circuits and electronics, signals and systems, digital electronics and computer architecture, electromagnetic waves, systems, and machinery, communications, and statistical mechanics.

Certification and Licensing

The Society of Cable Telecommunications Engineers and the International Association for Radio, Telecommunications and Electromagnetics offer certification for engineers employed in the telecommunications industry. Contact these organizations for more information.

Other Requirements

To be a successful electrical or electronics engineer, you should have strong problem-solving abilities, mathematical and scientific aptitudes, and the willingness to learn throughout one's career.

Most engineers work on teams with other professionals, and the ability to get along with others is essential. In addition, strong communications skills are needed. Engineers need to be able to write reports and give oral presentations.

EXPLORING

People who are interested in the excitement of electricity can tackle experiments such as building a radio or central processing unit of a computer. Special assignments can also be researched and supervised by teachers. Joining a science club, such as the Junior Engineering Technical Society (JETS), can provide hands-on activities and opportunities to explore scientific topics in depth. Student members can join competitions and design structures that exhibit scientific know-how. Reading publications, such as the *Pre-Engineering Times* (http://www.jets.org/newsletter), are other ways to learn about the engineering field. This magazine includes articles on engineering-related careers and club activities.

Students can also learn more about electrical and electronics engineering by attending a summer camp or academic program that focuses on scientific projects as well as recreational activities. Summer programs such as the one offered by the Michigan Technological University (http://www.mtu.edu) focus on career exploration in engineering, computers, electronics, and robotics. This academic program for high school students also offers arts guidance, wilderness events, and other recreational activities.

If you are interested in working in telecommunications, you should learn as much as you can about the industry as possible. Read industry publications such as *IEEE Wireless Communication Magazine* (http://www.comsoc.org/pubs/pcm) and *Communications Technology* (http://www.cable360.net/ct) and visit the Web sites of professional associations (see For More Information).

EMPLOYERS

More engineers work in the electrical and electronics field than in any other division of engineering. Most work in engineering and business consulting firms, manufacturing companies that produce electrical and electronic equipment, business machines, computers and data processing companies, and telecommunications parts. Others work for companies that make automotive electronics, scientific equipment, and aircraft parts; consulting firms; public utilities; and government agencies. Some work as private consultants.

Approximately 26,000 electrical and electronics engineers are employed in the U.S. telecommunications industry. In the telecommunications industry, major employers of electrical and electronics engineers include Qualcomm, AT&T, Verizon, Nokia, Sony, Comcast Cable Communications, Time Warner Cable, Cox Communications, DirecTV, and Dish Network Services.

STARTING OUT

Many students begin to research companies that they are interested in working for during their last year of college or even before. It is possible to research companies using many resources, such as company directories and annual reports, available at public libraries.

Employment opportunities can be found through a variety of sources. Many engineers are recruited by companies while they are still in college. Other companies have internship, work-study, or cooperative education programs from which they hire students who are still in college. Students who have participated in these programs often receive permanent job offers through these companies, or they may obtain useful contacts that can lead to a job interview or offer. Some companies use employment agencies and state employment offices. Companies may also advertise positions through advertisements in newspapers and trade publications. Professional associations—such as the Society of Cable Telecommunications Engineers and the International Association for Radio, Telecommunications and Electromagnetics—also offer job listings at their Web sites.

Interested applicants can also apply directly to a company they are interested in working for. A letter of interest and resume can be sent to the director of engineering or the head of a specific department. One may also apply to the personnel or human resources departments.

ADVANCEMENT

Engineering careers usually offer many avenues for advancement. An engineer straight out of college will usually take a job as an entry-level engineer and advance to higher positions after acquiring some job experience and technical skills. Engineers with strong technical skills who show leadership ability and good communications skills may move into positions that involve supervising teams of engineers and making sure they are working efficiently. Engineers can advance from these positions to that of a *chief engineer*. The chief engineer usually oversees all projects and has authority over project managers and managing engineers.

Many companies provide structured programs to train new employees and prepare them for advancement. These programs usually rely heavily on formal training opportunities such as in-house development programs and seminars. Some companies also provide special programs through colleges, universities, and outside agencies. Engineers usually advance from junior-level engineering positions to more senior-level positions through a series of positions. Engineers may also specialize in a specific area once they have acquired the necessary experience and skills.

Some engineers move into sales and managerial positions, with some engineers leaving the telecommunications industry to seek top-level management positions with other types of firms. Other engineers set up their own firms in design or consulting. Engineers can also move into the academic field and become teachers at high schools or universities.

The key to advancing in the electronics field is keeping pace with technological changes, which occur rapidly in this field. Electrical and electronics engineers will need to pursue additional training throughout their careers in order to stay up-to-date on new technologies and techniques.

EARNINGS

Starting salaries for engineers are generally much higher than for workers in any other field. According to a 2007 salary survey by the National Association of Colleges and Employers, graduates with a bachelor's degree in electrical/electronics and communications earned an average starting salary of $55,292. Those with a master's degree averaged around $66,309 in their first jobs after graduation, and those with a Ph.D. received average starting offers of $75,982.

The U.S. Department of Labor reports that the median annual salary for electronics engineers in the telecommunications industry was $73,382 in 2006. Salaries for all electronics engineers ranged from less than $52,050 to $119,900 or more annually. Electrical engineers employed in all industries earned salaries that ranged from less than $49,120 to $115,240 or more in 2006. Those employed in the telecommunications industry earned a mean salary of $74,170.

Most companies offer attractive benefits packages, although the actual benefits vary from company to company. Benefits can include any of the following: paid holidays, paid vacations, personal days, sick leave; medical, health, life insurance; short- and long-term disability insurance; profit sharing; 401(k) plans; retirement and pension plans; educational assistance; leave time for educational purposes; and credit unions. Some companies also offer computer purchase assistance plans and discounts on company products.

WORK ENVIRONMENT

For some employers, the five-day, 40-hour workweek is still the norm, but it is becoming much less common. Many engineers regularly work 10 or 20 hours of overtime a week. Engineers in research and development, or those conducting experiments, often need to work at night or on weekends. Workers who supervise production activities may need to come in during the evenings or on weekends to handle special production requirements. In addition to the time spent on the job, many engineers also participate in professional associations and pursue additional training during their free time. Many high-tech companies allow flex-time, which means that workers can arrange their own schedules within certain time frames.

Most electrical and electronics engineers work in fairly comfortable environments. Engineers involved in research and design may work in specially equipped laboratories. Engineers involved in development and manufacturing work in offices and may spend part of their time in production facilities. Depending on the type of work one does, there may be extensive travel. Engineers working for large telecommunications companies may travel to other plants and manufacturing companies, both around the country and at foreign locations.

OUTLOOK

Employment for electrical and electronics engineers in the telecommunications industry is expected to grow more slowly than the average for all occupations through 2016, according to the *Career Guide to Industries*. Despite this prediction, increases in computer and telecommunications production will create demand for skilled engineers.

Engineers will need to stay on top of changes within the electrical and electronics industry and will need additional training throughout their careers to learn new technologies. Economic trends and conditions within the global marketplace have become increasingly more important. In the past, most electronics production was done in the United States or by American-owned companies. During the 1990s, this changed, and the electronics industry entered an era of global production. Worldwide economies and production trends will have a larger impact on U.S. production, and companies that cannot compete technologically may not succeed. Job security is no longer a sure thing, and many engineers can expect to make significant changes in their careers at least once. Engineers who have a strong academic foundation, who have acquired technical knowledge and skills, and who stay up-to-date on changing technologies provide themselves with the versatility and flexibility to succeed within the electrical and electronics industry.

FOR MORE INFORMATION

For information on careers and educational programs, contact the following associations:

Institute of Electrical and Electronics Engineers
1828 L Street, NW, Suite 1202

Washington, DC 20036-5104
Tel: 202-785-0017
Email: ieeeusa@ieee.org
http://www.ieee.org

Electronic Industries Alliance
2500 Wilson Boulevard
Arlington, VA 22201-3834
Tel: 703-907-7500
http://www.eia.org

For information on certification, contact
**International Association for Radio, Telecommunications and
    Electromagnetics**
840 Queen Street
New Bern, NC 28560-4856
Tel: 800-89-NARTE
http://www.narte.org

*For information on careers, educational programs, and student
clubs, contact*
Junior Engineering Technical Society
1420 King Street, Suite 405
Alexandria, VA 22314-2794
Tel: 703-548-5387
Email: info@jets.org
http://www.jets.org

For information on careers and the cable industry, contact
National Cable & Telecommunications Association
25 Massachusetts Avenue, NW, Suite 100
Washington, DC 20001-1434
Tel: 202-222-2300
http://www.ncta.com

*For information on educational programs and job opportunities in
wireless technology (cellular, PCS, and satellite), contact*
Personal Communications Industry Association
901 North Washington Street, Suite 600
Alexandria VA 22314-1535
Tel: 800-759-0300
http://www.pcia.com

For information on careers, educational programs, educational seminars, distance learning, and certification, contact
Society of Cable Telecommunications Engineers
140 Philips Road
Exton, PA 19341-1318
Tel: 800-542-5040
Email: scte@scte.org
http://www.scte.org

―――――――――――――― **INTERVIEW** ――――――――――――――

Dr. Jay Porter is an associate professor and director of the Electronics Engineering Technology (EET) and Telecommunications Engineering Technology (TET) Programs at Texas A&M University in College Station, Texas. He has been with the Engineering Technology and Industrial Distribution Department at the university since 1998. Dr. Porter discussed the EET/TET programs and the education of engineering technology students with the editors of Careers in Focus: Telecommunications.

Q. Can you tell us about your program?

A. At Texas A&M University, we have two closely related engineering technology programs that service the needs of the telecommunications industry. Electronics Engineering Technology focuses on hardware and software development for modern electronic products, including products for the telecommunications industry. The Telecommunications Engineering Technology program's emphasis is on the design, development, and maintenance of small and large scale telecommunication systems. Both are four-year programs and are accredited by the Accreditation Board for Engineering and Technology. Because our programs are focused on undergraduate education and preparing students to enter the workforce directly out of college, we have a strong industrial advisory board that helps us maintain an up-to-date curriculum and identify trends in the industry. The industrial advisory board members are engineers/engineering managers and they meet with our faculty twice a year.

Because the Engineering Technology and Industrial Distribution Department is based in the Dwight Look College of Engineering, our faculty members not only focus on undergraduate education but also conduct applied research for regional and national industry. This means that our students have multiple opportunities to work on real industry projects while pursuing their education. In addition, both programs emphasize a multidisciplinary approach to education, ensuring that the students have in-class and extracurricular opportunities to interact with students from other engineering and business disciplines. Before graduating, all of our students participate in an industry-sponsored capstone design project, working in teams to design and implement new products and/or systems for the electronics and telecommunications industries.

Q. What is one thing that young people may not know about a career in telecommunications engineering technology (TET)?

A. Thirty years ago, most engineers and engineering technologists found employment with a large firm after graduation and more often than not, spent their entire career with that one company. Today, most engineering technology graduates entering the telecommunications workforce find that their career progression will include jobs with several different companies. Also, these moves typically come with a promotion and an increase in responsibility and salary.

Another exciting development for new telecommunications engineering technologists is the globalization of the industry. Graduates from our program find that they not only have job prospects across the nation, but that these opportunities often will allow them to travel internationally as well.

Q. For what type of jobs does your program prepare students?

A. The programs at Texas A&M University prepare students for a variety of positions in the telecommunications industry. These include positions in the areas of support and applications engineering, systems engineering, field engineering, and/or field service. A large number of our graduates are also hired as project managers to oversee both small- and large-scale telecommunications projects. Sectors of the telecommunications industry that hire our students include telecommunications product manufacturers, service providers, and telecommunications consulting firms. Large corporations that plan, install, and manage their own communication networks also employ our students.

Q. What are the most important personal and professional qualities for TET students?

A. Based on industry feedback, there are two qualities that are important for telecommunications engineering technology graduates. First, they must possess an in-depth technical knowledge of today's product and systems. For this reason, industry plays an important role in our curriculum and laboratory development process. It is essential that our students are being exposed to the most current technologies used in industry, as well as those technologies that we anticipate will be used two to five years in the future. Second, industry has told us that our graduates need to have strong project management and interpersonal/communication skills. Most of them will be working in teams on large projects, so being able to communicate, multitask, and manage their time and resources is extremely important.

Q. What is the employment outlook for the field? Have certain areas of this field been especially promising (or on the decline) in recent years?

A. Students graduating from our programs are all employed upon graduation, some having had multiple job offers. Most of our graduates take positions in either Texas or California, but many will have several opportunities to move to other areas across the United States and also around the world. One industry sector that used to hire a large percentage of our students was in the area of traditional telephony. However, with the decline of traditional telephone systems, we are seeing rapid growth in the areas of communications networking, digital communications (including data, voice, and video), and Voice over Internet Protocol.

Engineering Technicians

OVERVIEW

Engineering technicians use engineering, science, and mathematics to help engineers and other professionals in research and development, quality control, manufacturing, and many other fields. Approximately 511,000 engineering technicians are employed in the United States. Only a small percentage of all engineering technicians work in the telecommunications industry.

HISTORY

Engineering technicians assist engineers, scientists, and other workers in a variety of tasks. They are highly trained workers with strong backgrounds in a specialized technological field, such as civil, electrical, materials, and many other types of engineering. In short, engineering technicians can be found supporting engineers and other workers in any engineering discipline that comes to mind. They bridge the gap between the engineers who design the products, structures, and machines, and those who implement them. Engineering technicians have been valuable members of the engineering team ever since the first engineering projects were envisioned, planned, and implemented.

THE JOB

Many engineering technicians work for companies and contractors in the telecommunications industry, namely, cable, wire line and cellular telephone, and the Internet. Their duties vary according to their particular field.

Civil engineering technicians help in the collection, data analysis, and planning for the construction of structures needed in the transmission of telecommunication signals. Technicians employed at Comcast, for example, may help in the design, construction, and installation of towers and antennas or utility houses. They may also be involved in the planning of location, and the construction of trenches in which to lay cables and conduits.

Electrical and electronics engineering technicians help engineers design, test, improve, and repair electronic equipment and devices. For example, technicians working at Lucent Technologies may be involved in projects such as fine tuning or testing switches, capacitors, or other components found in circuit boards and other telecommunications equipment. Electronic and electrical engineers may work in subspecialties such as electronics development, electronic drafting, electronics manufacturing and production, service, and maintenance.

Mechanical engineering technicians assist a team of engineers and other professionals in the design, manufacturing, and testing of different machines, mechanical devices, tools, and accessories used in the telecommunications industry. For example, technicians at Nokia may help design future models of cellular phones. Their work makes it possible for these cellular phones to be sleeker, smaller, and have the capacity to access the Internet and play music and videos, among other features.

Industrial engineering technicians assist industrial engineers in their duties: they collect and analyze data and make recommendations for the efficient use of personnel, materials, and machines to produce goods or to provide services. They may study the time, movements, and methods a worker uses to accomplish daily tasks in production, maintenance, or clerical areas. The kind of work done by industrial engineering technicians varies, depending on the size and type of company for which they work. A variety of subspecialties are available, including methods engineering technicians, materials handling technicians, plant layout technicians, work measurement technicians, time-study technicians, production-control technicians, and inventory control technicians.

Some *materials engineering technicians* specialize in fiber optics communication, which uses light in the form of glass or plastic optical fiber bundles to transmit information quickly over great distances. Companies that transmit digital information using fiber optics include telephone carriers, cable television companies, and Internet carriers.

Robotics engineering technicians assist robotics engineers in a wide variety of tasks relating to the design, development, production, testing, operation, repair, and maintenance of telecommunications equipment and robotic devices.

Engineering technicians work in a variety of conditions depending on their field of specialization. Technicians who specialize in design may find that they spend most of their time at the drafting board or computer. Those who specialize in manufacturing may spend some time at a desk but also spend considerable time in manufacturing areas or shops.

REQUIREMENTS

High School

You will need a minimum of an associate's degree to work in this field. Preparation for this career begins in high school. Although entrance requirements to associate's degree programs vary somewhat from school to school, mathematics and physical science form the backbone of a good preparatory curriculum. Classes should include algebra, geometry, science, trigonometry, calculus, chemistry, mechanical drawing, shop, and physics. Because computers have become essential for engineering technicians, computer courses are also important.

English and speech courses provide invaluable experience in improving verbal and written communication skills. Since some technicians go on to become technical writers or teachers, and since all of these occupations require the ability to explain technical matters clearly and concisely, you will need to develop solid written and verbal communication skills in high school.

Postsecondary Training

While some current engineering technicians have entered the field without formal academic training, it is increasingly difficult to do so. Most employers are interested in hiring graduates with at least a two-year degree in engineering technology. Technical institutes, community colleges, vocational schools, and universities all offer this course of study.

The Technology Accreditation Commission of the Accreditation Board for Engineering and Technology (http://www.abet.org) accredits engineering technology programs.

Some engineering technicians decide to pursue advancement in their field by becoming engineering technologists. Others decide to branch off into research and development or become engineers. These higher-level and higher-paid positions typically require the completion of a bachelor's degree in engineering technology for engineering technologists or at least a bachelor's degree in engineering for technicians interested in working in research and development or becoming engineers.

Certification or Licensing

Certification and licensing requirements vary by specialty. Check with your state's department of labor and telecommunications associations for further information.

Many engineering technicians choose to become certified by the National Institute for Certification in Engineering Technologies. To become certified, you must combine a specific amount of job-related experience with a written examination. Certifications are offered at several levels of expertise. Such certification is generally voluntary, although obtaining certification shows a high level of commitment and dedication that employers find highly desirable.

Electronics engineering technicians may obtain voluntary certification from the International Society of Certified Electronics Technicians, the Electronics Technicians Association International, and the International Association for Radio, Telecommunications and Electromagnetics. Certification is regarded as a demonstration of professional dedication, determination, and know-how.

Engineering technicians are encouraged to become affiliated with professional groups, such as the American Society of Certified Engineering Technicians, that offer continuing education sessions for members. Additionally, some engineering technicians may be required to belong to unions.

Other Requirements

All engineering technicians are relied upon for solutions and must express their ideas clearly in speech and in writing. Good communication skills are important for a technician in the writing and presenting of reports and plans. These skills are also important for working alongside other technicians and professionals, people who are often from many different backgrounds and skilled in varying areas of engineering.

Engineering technicians need mathematical and mechanical aptitude. They must understand abstract concepts and apply scientific principles to problems in the shop, laboratory, or work site.

Many tasks assigned to engineering technicians require patience and methodical, persistent work. Good technicians work well with their hands, paying close attention to every detail of a project. Some technicians are bored by the repetitiveness of some tasks, while others enjoy the routine.

Other Opportunities in the Telecommunications Industry

In addition to the careers covered in this book, there are a variety of other options in the telecommunications industry, including:

Accountants and Auditors

Bill and Account Collectors

Bookkeeping, Accounting, and Auditing Clerks

Budget Analysts

Business Executives

Computer Programmers

Computer Specialists

Computer Systems Analysts

Cost Estimators

Credit Analysts

Electricians

Financial Analysts

Human Resources Managers

Industrial Machinery Mechanics

Industrial Truck and Tractor Operators

Information Systems Managers

Laborers and Hand Freight, Stock, and Material Movers

Lawyers

Logisticians

Office Managers

Paralegals

Plumbers and Pipefitters

Public Relations Specialists

Purchasing Agents

Receptionists

Secretaries

Security Guards

Telecommunications Historians

Individuals planning to advance beyond the technician's level should be willing to and capable of pursuing some form of higher education.

EXPLORING

If you are interested in a career as an engineering technician, you can gain relevant experience by taking shop courses, joining electronics or radio clubs in school, and assembling electronic equipment with commercial kits.

You should take every opportunity to discuss the field with people working in it. Try to visit a variety of different kinds of engineering facilities—service shops, manufacturing plants, and research laboratories—either through individual visits or through field trips organized by teachers or guidance counselors. These visits will provide a realistic idea of the opportunities in the different areas of the telecommunications industry. If you enroll in a community college or technical school, you may be able to secure off-quarter or part-time internships with local employers through your school's career services office. Internships are a valuable way to gain experience while still in school.

EMPLOYERS

Approximately 511,000 engineering technicians are employed in the United States. Only a small percentage of the total number of engineering technicians are employed in the telecommunications industry. Engineering technicians work for all major telecommunications companies including Qualcomm, AT&T, Verizon, Motorola, Nokia, Sony, Comcast Cable Communications, Time Warner Cable, Cox Communications, DirecTV, and Dish Network Services.

STARTING OUT

Most technical schools, community colleges, and universities have career services offices. Telecommunications companies actively recruit employees while they are still in school or are nearing graduation. Because these job services are the primary source of entry-level jobs for engineering technicians, you should check out a school's placement rate for your specific field before making a final decision about attending.

Another way to obtain employment is through direct contact with a particular telecommunications company. It is best to write to the personnel department and include a resume summarizing your education and experience. If the company has an appropriate opening, a company representative will schedule an interview with you. There are also many excellent public and commercial employment organizations that can help graduates obtain jobs appropriate to their training and experience.

Newspaper want ads and employment services are other methods of getting jobs. Professional or trade magazines often have job listings and can be good sources for job seekers. Professional associations compile information on job openings and publish job lists. For example, the International Society of Certified Electronics Technicians offers lists of job openings around the country at its Web site. Information about job openings can also be found in trade magazines. Professional organizations are also good for networking with other technicians and are up to date on industry advancement, changes, and areas of employment.

ADVANCEMENT

As engineering technicians remain with a company, they become more valuable to the employer. Opportunities for advancement are available for engineering technicians who are willing to accept greater responsibilities either by specializing in a specific field, taking on more technically complex assignments, or by assuming supervisory duties. Some technicians advance by moving into technical sales or customer relations. Others pursue advanced education to become engineering technologists or engineers.

EARNINGS

The earnings of engineering technicians vary widely depending on skills and experience, the type of work, geographical location, and other factors. The U.S. Department of Labor reports the following mean salaries for engineering technicians employed in the telecommunications industry by specialty in 2006: civil, $65,730; electrical and electronics, $53,780; and all other engineering specialties, $61,460. Salaries for engineering technicians employed in all industries ranged from less than $24,000 to $76,000 or more annually.

Engineering technicians generally receive premium pay for overtime work on Sundays and holidays and for evening and night-shift work. Most employers offer benefits packages that include paid holidays, paid vacations, sick days, and health insurance. Companies may also offer pension and retirement plans, profit sharing, 401(k) plans, tuition assistance programs, and release time for additional education.

WORK ENVIRONMENT

Depending on their jobs, engineering technicians may work in the shop or office areas or in both. The type of plant facilities depends on the product. For example, a plant producing microchips for cell phones requires very clean working conditions. Technicians employed in manufacturing may work in loud, busy settings.

Engineering technicians often travel to other locations or areas. They may accompany engineers to technical conventions or on visits to other companies to gain insight into new or different methods of operation and production.

Continuing education plays a large role in the life of engineering technicians. They may attend classes or seminars, keeping up-to-date with emerging technology and methods of managing production efficiently.

Hours of work may vary and depend on factory shifts. Engineering technicians are often asked to get jobs done quickly and to meet very tight deadlines.

OUTLOOK

According to the *Occupational Outlook Handbook (OOH)*, employment of electrical and electronics engineering technicians—one of the largest technician specialties in the telecommunications industry—is expected to grow more slowly than the average for all occupations through 2016. Computer-aided design allows individual technicians to increase productivity, thereby limiting job growth. Those with training in sophisticated technologies and those with degrees in technology will have the best employment opportunities.

For all industries, the *OOH* reports the following employment outlooks for engineering technicians by specialty: civil, about as fast as the average; electrical and electronics, more slowly than the average; industrial, about as fast as the average; and mechanical, more slowly than the average.

FOR MORE INFORMATION

Visit the ASEE's precollege Web site for information on engineering and engineering technology careers.
American Society for Engineering Education (ASEE)
1818 N Street, NW, Suite 600
Washington, DC 20036-2479
Tel: 202-331-3500
Email: outreach@asee.org
http://www.engineeringk12.org/students/default.php

Contact the society for information on training and certification.
American Society of Certified Engineering Technicians
PO Box 1536

Brandon, MS 39043-1536
Tel: 601-824-8991
Email: general-manager@ascet.org
http://www.ascet.org

This organization offers information on certification and student membership.
Electronics Technicians Association International
5 Depot Street
Greencastle, IN 46135-8024
Tel: 800-288-3824
Email: eta@eta-i.org
http://www.eta-i.org

For information on certification, contact
International Association for Radio, Telecommunications and Electromagnetics
840 Queen Street
New Bern, NC 28560-4856
Tel: 800-896-2783
http://www.narte.org

Contact the society for information on certification and student membership.
International Society of Certified Electronics Technicians
3608 Pershing Avenue
Fort Worth, TX 76107-4527
Tel: 817-921-9101
Email: info@iscet.org
http://www.iscet.org

For information on careers, educational programs, and student clubs, contact
Junior Engineering Technical Society
1420 King Street, Suite 405
Alexandria, VA 22314-2794
Tel: 703-548-5387
Email: info@jets.org
http://www.jets.org

For information on careers and the cable industry, contact
National Cable & Telecommunications Association
25 Massachusetts Avenue, NW, Suite 100
Washington, DC 20001-1434

Tel: 202-222-2300
http://www.ncta.com

For information on educational programs and job opportunities in wireless technology (cellular, PCS, and satellite), contact
Personal Communications Industry Association
901 North Washington Street, Suite 600
Alexandria VA 22314-1535
Tel: 800-759-0300
http://www.pcia.com

Fiber Optics Technicians

QUICK FACTS

School Subjects
Mathematics
Technical/shop

Personal Skills
Mechanical/manipulative
Technical/scientific

Work Environment
Indoors and outdoors
Primarily multiple locations

Minimum Education Level
High school diploma

Salary Range
$24,700 to $50,000 to
$68,220+

Certification or Licensing
Voluntary

Outlook
More slowly than the average

DOT
N/A

GOE
05.02.01

NOC
7246

O*NET-SOC
49-9052.00

OVERVIEW

Fiber optics technicians work with the optical fibers and cables used in transmitting communications data. Depending on the area of employment, technicians splice fibers, fuse fibers together, and install fiber cables beneath ground and in buildings. These technicians work for telephone and cable companies, and other businesses involved in telecommunications.

HISTORY

A need to convey messages quickly led to experimentation in the use of light to communicate. Before the introduction of the electric telegraph in the mid-1800s, a series of semaphores atop towers allowed for communication between tower operators. Ships also used light signals to communicate with each other. But the reliability of wires to carry electricity, and the invention of the electric telegraph and the telephone, put the further development of optical communications on hold.

Studies in the field of medicine led to the discovery that rods of glass or plastic could carry light. In the 1950s, these developments helped such engineers as Alec Reeves of Great Britain in the experimentation of fiber optics for telecommunications. Increasing television and telephone use demanded more transmission bandwidth, and the invention of the laser in 1960 made optical communications a reality. Technical barriers remained, however, and experimentation continued for many years, leading to the first telephone field trials in 1977. Today, the career of fiber optics technician is instrumental to communications, as telecommunications companies recognize the importance of fiber optics in the future of high-speed, high-definition service. Most phone connections made today are over fiber optic cables. The Internet is also transmitted by fiber optics.

THE JOB

Fiber optics technicians prepare, install, and test fiber optics transmission systems. These systems are composed of fiber optic cables and allow for data communication between computers, phones, and faxes. When working for a telecommunications company, fiber optics technicians are often required to install lines for local area networks—these data networks serve small areas of linked computers, such as in an office.

The telecommunications company for which a technician works will contract with a company to create a communications system. A sales worker will evaluate the customer's needs, and then order the materials for the installation. Fiber optics technicians take these materials to the job site. Each job site may be very different—technicians may work in a variety of different locales. First, fiber optics technicians need to get a sense of the area. They walk through with the client, evaluating the areas where they will be installing fiber optic cable. Newer buildings will be readily equipped for installation; in some older buildings, it may be more difficult to get behind ceiling tiles and in the walls.

After they have readied the area for cable, fiber optics technicians run the cable from the computer's mainframe to individual workstations. They then test the cable, using power meters and other devices, by running a laser through it. Fiber optics technicians use equipment that measures the amount of time it takes for the laser to go through, determining any signal loss or faults in the fiber link.

Technicians may also fuse fibers together. This involves cleaning the fiber and cutting it with a special diamond-headed cleaver. After they have prepared both ends, they place them into a fusion splicer. At the press of a button, the splicer fuses the two fibers together.

REQUIREMENTS

High School

There are not really any specific high school courses that will prepare you for work as a fiber optics technician, but shop classes will give you experience working with tools to complete a variety of projects, speech and writing classes will help you improve your communication skills, and mathematics classes will prepare you to work with computations and installation plans.

Postsecondary Training

A college degree is not required but can give you an edge when looking for work as a fiber optics technician. A number of community colleges across the country offer programs in fiber optics technology or broadband networks technology. These programs offer such courses as cable construction, fiber optic installation techniques, singlemode and multimode systems, and wavelength and bandwidth. They also may include lab and certification components. Short-term training opportunities, lasting only a few days, may also be available at some schools.

Certification or Licensing

The Fiber Optic Association offers the following voluntary certifications: certified fiber optic technician, certified FTTx technician (for technicians who connect fiber to customers' premises or home), advanced fiber optic technician, certified fiber optic specialist, and certified fiber optic instructor. The Electronics Technicians Association International offers several certifications in fiber optics. The Telecommunications Industry Association offers a certification program for technicians working in convergence technologies, and the International Association for Radio, Telecommunications and Electromagnetics offers certification for technicians employed in the telecommunications industry.

Other Requirements

Because of the fine nature of the fibers, you should have a steady hand and good eyesight in assembling fiber optic cables. You will also need good math skills for working with detailed plans and designs. Some companies may require you to have your own special fiber optic tools.

EXPLORING

Visit the Web sites of the associations listed at the end of this article to learn more about the industry. Ask a teacher to set up an interview with an experienced fiber optics technician. Talking with someone in the field is the best way to learn the pros and cons of any career.

Technicians lay fiber optic cable. *(James Leynse, Corbis)*

EMPLOYERS

Fiber optics technicians work for telephone companies, cable companies, and computer networking businesses. They may also work as freelancers, hiring on with companies on special installation projects.

STARTING OUT

There are many sources of information about developments in fiber optics and the telecommunications industry, including professional associations and Web sites. When you complete a fiber optics technology program, your school will be able to direct you to local job opportunities. Information Gatekeepers publishes the *Optical Networks/Fiber Optics Yellow Pages*, a directory that lists more than 1,000 companies. For more information, visit Information Gatekeepers' Web site, http://www.igigroup.com.

ADVANCEMENT

Even without special fiber optics training, fiber optics technicians may be able to enter the job market in an entry-level position with a telecommunications company. The company may have its own training program, or offer tuition reimbursement for outside seminars in fiber optics technology. After they've gained experience working with fiber optic cable, fiber optics technicians may be able to move into a management or executive position. They may also become consultants, advising companies on data transmission problems.

EARNINGS

The U.S. Department of Labor reports the following: median annual earnings for telecommunications line installers and repairers (which include those who work with fiber optics) by employer in 2006: satellite communications, $57,640; wired telecommunications carriers, $55,620; telecommunications resellers, $54,420; cable and other subscription programming, $39,720; and cable and other program distribution, $38,800. Salaries for all line installers and repairers ranged from less than $24,700 to $68,220 or more per year.

Companies offer a variety of benefit packages, which can include any of the following: paid holidays, vacations, and sick days; personal days; medical, dental, and life insurance; profit-sharing plans; 401(k) plans; retirement and pension plans; and educational assistance programs.

WORK ENVIRONMENT

Fiber optics technicians who work as assemblers spend most of their time sitting at a bench. Technicians who work as installers usually work out in the field installing fiber beneath the ground. There is little physical exertion required because machinery is used to dig the trenches. Fiber optics technicians spend part of their time outside repairing fiber, and part of their time in a van preparing the fibers for installation. They may also install fiber cables in buildings; this will require some climbing of ladders and working beneath floorboards.

OUTLOOK

The U.S. Department of Labor projects that employment of telecommunications line installers and repairers will grow more slowly than the average for all occupations through 2016. The growth of wireless and satellite communications technologies for use in the delivery of communications, video, and data services will limit job growth in the field.

Digital transmissions will soon be the norm for telecommunications—not only do modern offices require data communications systems, but cable companies are investing in fiber optics to offer digital TV and cable, as well as quality phone service. Also, the cost of fiber is dropping, which means more companies will invest in fiber optics. As a result, experienced fiber optics assemblers and installers will find job opportunities. Additionally, strong employment opportunities should be available for fiber optics technicians who work for telephone companies connecting fiber from exterior lines to customer's homes or to businesses. The Fiber Optic Association reports that major phone companies are "committing billions of dollars to plans for connecting millions of homes and offices with fiber in the future."

FOR MORE INFORMATION

For information on certification, contact
Electronics Technicians Association International
5 Depot Street
Greencastle, IN 46135-8024
Tel: 800-288-3824
Email: eta@tds.net
http://www.eta-i.org

To learn about certification and approved training programs, contact
Fiber Optic Association
1119 South Mission Road, #355
Fallbrook, CA 92028-3225
Tel: 760-451-3655
Email: info@thefoa.org
http://www.thefoa.org

For information on certification, contact
International Association for Radio, Telecommunications and Electromagnetics
840 Queen Street
New Bern, NC 28560-4856
Tel: 800-896-2783
http://www.narte.org

To learn about telecommunications technology and uses for fiber optics, visit the OSA Web site.
Optical Society of America (OSA)
2010 Massachusetts Avenue, NW
Washington, DC 20036-1012
Tel: 202-223-8130
Email: info@osa.org

http://www.osa.org

For information on certification, contact
Telecommunications Industry Association
2500 Wilson Boulevard, Suite 300
Arlington, VA 22201-3834
Tel: 703-907-7700
http://www.tiaonline.org

To learn about opportunities for women in the fiber optics industry, contact
Women in Cable Telecommunications
14555 Avion Parkway, Suite 250
Chantilly, VA 20151-1117
Tel: 703-234-9810
http://www.wict.org

For information on educational programs in optics, visit
Optics Education: International Directory of Degree Programs
   in Optics
Email: opticsed@spie.org
http://www.opticseducation.org

Industrial Designers

OVERVIEW

Industrial designers combine technical knowledge of materials, machines, and production with artistic talent to improve the appearance and function of machine-made products—including those produced by the telecommunications industry. There are approximately 48,000 industrial designers employed in the United States. Only a small percentage work in the telecommunications industry.

HISTORY

Although industrial design as a separate and unique profession did not develop in the United States until the 1920s, it has its origins in colonial America and the industrial revolution. When colonists were faced with having to make their own products rather than relying on imported goods, they learned to modify existing objects and create new ones. As the advent of the industrial revolution drew near, interest in machinery and industry increased.

One of the earliest examples of industrial design is found in Eli Whitney's production of muskets. In 1800, he promised to manufacture several thousand muskets for the government using the principles of standardization and interchangeable parts. Designs and manufacturing processes for each musket part had to be created. This early example of industrial design involved not only designing an individual product but also the manufacturing processes and the production equipment.

The Industrial Revolution brought about the mass production of objects and increased machine manufacturing. As production capabilities grew, a group of entrepreneurs, inventors, and designers emerged. Together, these individuals developed products that could be mass-produced and figured out ways to manufacture them.

In the early 1900s, the number of products available to the public grew, as did the purchasing power of individuals. Manufacturers realized that in order to compete with imported goods and skilled craftpersons, they needed to offer a wide variety of products that were well designed and affordable. At that time, manufactured products were designed to be functional, utilitarian, and easily produced by machines. Little attention was paid to aesthetics. Product designs were copied from imported items, and there was little original design.

Consumers were growing increasingly dissatisfied with the products they were offered. They felt that machine-made goods were, in many cases, ugly and unattractive. Manufacturers did not initially respond to these complaints. For example, Henry Ford continued to manufacture only one style of car, the Model T, despite criticism that it looked like a tin can. Ford was unconcerned because he sold more cars than anyone else. When General Motors started selling its attractive Chevrolet in 1926, and it outsold the Ford, he finally recognized the importance of styling and design.

Advertising convincingly demonstrated the importance of design. Those products with artistic features sold better, and manufacturers realized that design did play an important role both in marketing and manufacturing. By 1927, manufacturers were hiring people solely to advise them on design features. Industrial design came to represent a new profession: The practice of using aesthetic design features to create manufactured goods that were economical, served a specific purpose, and satisfied the psychological needs of consumers. Most of the early industrial designers came from Europe until design schools were established in America.

Industrial design as a profession grew rapidly in the years from 1927 until World War II. Many of the early industrial designers established their own firms rather than working directly for a manufacturer. After the war, consumer goods proliferated, which helped the field continue to grow. Manufacturers paid more attention to style and design in an effort to make their products stand out in the marketplace. They began to hire in-house designers. Today, industrial designers, including those in the telecommunications industry, play a significant role in both designing new products and determining which products may be successful in the marketplace.

THE JOB

Industrial designers in the telecommunications industry play an integral role in the manufacturing process. They create designs for new products (such as cell phones and PDAs) and redesign existing products. Before a product can be manufactured, a design must be created that specifies its form, function, and appearance. Industrial designers must pay attention to the purpose of the proposed product, anticipate differentiated use by specific consumers (for example, a cell phone model that is typically used by teenagers, a PDA that is used for business meetings, etc.), and keep in mind the economic factors affecting its design and manufacture, materials used, and safety requirements.

Industrial designers usually work as part of a team that includes engineers, marketing specialists, production personnel, sales representatives, and sometimes, top manufacturing managers. Before the design process actually begins, market research or surveys may be conducted that analyze how well a product is performing, what its market share is, and how well competitors' products are doing. In addition, feasibility studies may be conducted to determine whether an existing design should be changed or a new product created to keep or gain market share. For example, the maker of ultra-slim cell phones might conduct a survey to determine how users prefer the phone in terms of appearance, usability, and overall functionality. If the responses suggest that the design needs improvement, designers may increase the size of the touchpad, create new color choices, and otherwise revise the product to ensure their company retains market share.

Once a determination is made to create a new design, an industrial designer is assigned to the project. The designer reviews study results and meets with other design team members to develop a concept. The designer studies the features of the proposed product as well as the material requirements and manufacturing costs and requirements. Several designs are sketched and other team members are consulted.

Some designers still create sketches by hand, but most use design software that allows them to create sketches on a computer. Once a preliminary design is selected, designers work out all of the details. They calculate all of the measurements of each part of the design, identify specific components, select necessary materials (such as types of metal and plastic for wired or wireless phones), and choose colors and other visual elements. A detailed design is then submitted to engineers and other design team members for review.

In some cases, a model or prototype may be built; however, computer-aided design programs now allow engineers to test design features before this stage. Engineers test for performance, strength, durability, and other factors to ensure that a product actually performs as planned and meets all safety and industrial standards. If any part of a product fails to meet test standards, the design is sent back to the industrial designer for revisions.

This process continues until the design passes all test stages. At this point, a model may be built of clay, foam, wood, or other materials to serve as a guide for production. In some cases, a prototype made of the actual materials and components will be built. The design, along with all computer data and any models and prototypes, is then turned over to the production department, which is responsible for the manufacture of the prototype.

Industrial designers may also become involved in the marketing and advertising promotion of products. They may name the new product, design the product's packaging, plan promotional campaigns or advertising strategies, and create artwork used for advertising.

Industrial designers may design the layout of retail sales offices of telecommunications companies so that these offices present a coordinated company image. This type of design can also include developing company symbols, trademarks, and logos.

Designers may work for a design firm or directly for a telecommunications company. They may freelance or set up their own consulting firms. Corporate designers may be part of a large team with designers at various locations. Computer networking allows several designers to work simultaneously on the same project. Using this approach, a designer creates one part of a design, for example, the electronic components, while another designer creates another part, such as the mechanical housing. A variation on the multidesigner approach schedules designers on different shifts to work on the same project.

Technology is changing the way industrial designers work. Computer-aided industrial design tools are revolutionizing the way products are designed and manufactured. These programs allow designers and engineers to test products during the design stage so that design flaws are identified before prototypes are built. Other programs allow product models to be tested online. Designs can be sent directly to machine tools that produce three-dimensional models. All of these advances decrease the time necessary to design a product, test it, and manufacture it.

REQUIREMENTS

High School
In high school, take as many art and computer classes as possible in addition to college preparatory classes in English, social studies, algebra, geometry, and science. Classes in mechanical drawing may

be helpful, but drafting skills are being replaced by the ability to use computers to create graphics and manipulate objects. Science classes, such as physics and chemistry, are also becoming more important as industrial designers select materials and components for products and need to have a basic understanding of scientific principles. Shop classes, such as machine shop, metalworking, and woodworking, are also useful and provide training in using hand and machine tools.

Postsecondary Training

A bachelor's degree in fine arts or industrial design is recommended, although some employers accept diplomas from art schools. Training is offered through art schools, art departments of colleges and universities, and technical colleges. Most bachelor's degree programs require four or five years to complete. Some schools also offer a master's degree, which requires two years of additional study. Often, art schools grant a diploma for three years of study in industrial design. Programs in industrial design are offered by approximately 50 schools accredited (or that are in the process of accreditation) by the National Association of Schools of Art and Design.

School programs vary; some emphasize engineering and technical work, while, others emphasize art background. Certain basic courses are common to every school: two-dimensional design (color theory, spatial organization) and three-dimensional design (abstract sculpture, art structures). Students also have a great deal of studio practice, learning to make models of clay, plaster, wood, and other easily worked materials. Some schools even use metalworking machinery. Technically oriented schools generally require a course in basic engineering. Schools offering degree programs also require courses in English, history, science, and other basic subjects. Such courses as merchandising and business are important for anyone working in a field so closely connected with the consumer such as in the telecommunications industry. Most schools also offer classes in computer-aided design and computer graphics. One of the most essential skills for success as an industrial designer is the ability to use design software.

Other Requirements

Industrial designers are creative, have artistic ability, and are able to work closely with others in a collaborative style. In general, designers do not crave fame or recognition because designing is a joint project involving the skills of many people. In most cases, industrial designers remain anonymous and behind the scenes. Successful designers can accept criticism and differences of opinion and be open to new ideas.

EXPLORING

An excellent way to uncover an aptitude for design and to gain practical experience in using computers is to take a computer graphics course through an art school, high school continuing education program, technical school, or community college. Some community colleges allow high school students to enroll in classes if no comparable course is offered at the high school level. If no formal training is available, teach yourself how to use a popular graphics software package.

Summer or part-time employment in an industrial design office is a good way to learn more about the profession and what industrial designers do. Another option is to work in an advertising agency or for a market research firm, ideally, one that consults for a telecommunications company. Although these companies most likely won't have an industrial designer on staff, they will provide exposure to how to study consumer trends and plan marketing promotions.

Pursue hobbies such as sculpting, ceramics, jewelry making, woodworking, and sketching to develop creative and artistic abilities. Reading about industrial design can also be very beneficial. Publications such as *Design News* (http://www.designnews.com) contain many interesting and informative articles that describe different design products and report on current trends. This magazine can be found at many public libraries. Read books on the history of industrial design to learn about interesting case studies on the development of specific products.

EMPLOYERS

Approximately 48,000 industrial designers are employed in the United States, with only a small percentage of this total employed in the telecommunications industry. Industrial designers work in all areas of industry. Some specialize in consumer products, such as cell phones and PDAs, household appliances, home entertainment items, personal computers, clothing, jewelry, and car stereos. Others work in designing automobiles, electronic devices, airplanes, biomedical products, medical equipment, measuring instruments, or office equipment. Most designers specialize in a specific area of manufacturing and work on only a few types of products.

STARTING OUT

Most employers prefer to hire someone who has a degree or diploma from a college, art school, or technical school. Persons with engineering, architectural, or other scientific backgrounds also have a good chance at entry-level jobs, especially if they have artistic and creative talent. When interviewing for a job, a designer should be prepared to present a portfolio of work.

Job openings may be listed through a college career services office or in classified ads in newspapers or trade magazines. Qualified beginners may also apply directly to companies that hire industrial designers. Several directories listing industrial design firms can be found in most public libraries. In addition, lists of industrial design firms appear periodically in magazines such as *BusinessWeek* and *Engineering News-Record*. In addition, a new industrial designer can get a free copy of *Getting an Industrial Design Job* at the Web site (http://www.idsa.org) of the Industrial Designers Society of America.

ADVANCEMENT

Entry-level industrial designers usually begin as assistants to other designers. They do routine work and hold little responsibility for design changes. With experience and the necessary qualifications, the designer may be promoted to a higher-ranking position with major responsibility for design. Experienced designers may be promoted to project managers or move into supervisory positions. Supervisory positions may include overseeing and coordinating the work of several designers, including freelancers and industrial designers working at outside agencies. Some senior designers are given a free hand in designing products. By gaining experience, establishing a reputation for excellence and reliability, and obtaining financial backing, some industrial designers decide to open their own consulting firms.

EARNINGS

According to the Industrial Designers Society of America, the average starting salary for industrial designers is $36,000. Designers with five years' experience earn an average of $58,000 a year. Senior designers with 10 years' experience earn $73,000. Industrial designers with 19 years or more experience earn average salaries of $125,000. Managers who direct design departments in large companies earn substantially more income. Owners or partners of consulting firms have fluctuating incomes, depending on their business for the year.

According to the U.S. Department of Labor, industrial designers earned a median annual salary of $54,560 in 2006. The lowest 10 percent earned less than $31,510 annually, and the top 10 percent earned more than $92,970.

Industrial designers usually receive paid vacations and holidays, sick leave, hospitalization and insurance benefits, and pension programs.

WORK ENVIRONMENT

Industrial designers enjoy generally pleasant working conditions. In many companies, the atmosphere is relaxed and casual. Most designers spend a significant amount of time at either a computer workstation or drawing board. Most industrial designers work at least 40 hours a week, with overtime frequently required. There is a lot of pressure to speed up the design/development process and get products to market as soon as possible. For some designers, this can mean regularly working 10 to 20 hours or more of overtime a week. Working on weekends and into the evening can be required to run a special computer program or to work on a project with a tight deadline. Designers who freelance, or work for themselves, set their own hours but may work more than 40 hours a week in order to meet the needs of their clients.

OUTLOOK

The U.S. Department of Labor predicts that employment in the telecommunications industry will grow more slowly than the average for all industries through 2016. Despite this prediction, there should be steady employment opportunities for industrial designers since they play such an important role in the success of companies in the field.

Employment of industrial designers in all industries is expected to grow about as fast as the average through 2016, according to the U.S. Department of Labor (USDL). This favorable outlook is based on the need to improve product quality and safety, to design new products for the global marketplace, and to design high-technology products in consumer electronics, medicine, and transportation. The USDL predicts that designers who combine business expertise with an educational background in engineering and computer-aided design will have the best employment prospects.

Despite the demand for industrial designers, many companies prefer to outsource a significant amount of their work. This is a growing trend within the industry that may make it more difficult for a beginning worker to find an entry-level job. In addition, this is a profession that is somewhat influenced by the economic climate. It thrives in times of prosperity and declines in periods of recession.

FOR MORE INFORMATION

For information on opportunities for women in industrial design, contact
  Association of Women Industrial Designers
  Old Chelsea Station
  PO Box 468
  New York, NY 10011
  Email: info@awidweb.com
  http://www.awidweb.com

For information on careers, educational programs, and a free copy of Getting an Industrial Design Job, *contact*
  Industrial Designers Society of America
  45195 Business Court, Suite 250
  Dulles, VA 20166-6717
  Tel: 703-707-6000
  Email: idsa@idsa.org
  http://www.idsa.org

For information on accredited design schools, contact
  National Association of Schools of Art and Design
  11250 Roger Bacon Drive, Suite 21
  Reston, VA 20190-5248
  Tel: 703-437-0700
  Email: info@arts-accredit.org
  http://nasad.arts-accredit.org

Line Installers and Cable Splicers

QUICK FACTS

School Subjects
Mathematics
Technical/shop

Personal Skills
Following instructions
Mechanical/manipulative

Work Environment
Primarily outdoors
Primarily multiple locations

Minimum Education Level
High school diploma

Salary Range
$24,700 to $50,000 to
$68,220+

Certification or Licensing
Voluntary

Outlook
More slowly than the average

DOT
821

GOE
05.01.02

NOC
N/A

O*NET-SOC
49-9052.00

OVERVIEW

Line installers and cable splicers construct, maintain, and repair the vast network of wires and cables that transmit telephone, cable television, the Internet, and electric power lines to commercial and residential customers. Line construction and cable splicing is a vital part of the communications system. Workers are involved in linking electricity between generation plants and homes and other buildings, merging phone communications between telephone central offices and customers, and bringing cable television stations to residences and other locations. There are approximately 275,000 line installers and cable splicers working in the United States. About 59 percent work in the telecommunications industry.

HISTORY

The occupation of line installers and cable splicers is related to major developments in electromagnetic technology since the late 19th century. The roots of this technology are traced to 1831, when Michael Faraday discovered electric induction. In the late 1880s came the invention and patents for the incandescent lamp, and by the turn of the century electric lighting was a common phenomenon throughout urban areas.

The generation of electricity took on further commercial significance as the telecommunications industry was born after Alexander Graham Bell's patent of the telephone in 1876. During the first quarter of the 20th century, the electronics industry focused on communications and broadcast entertainment. As the need developed for more and more telephone lines to connect distant points throughout the country, line installers and cable splicers were trained and employed to construct and maintain these lines.

After World War II, the television started to become a common addition in homes around the country. In the 1950s, cable television systems were designed for better reception of network broadcasts in remote areas, and by the 1970s such systems were becoming familiar to residential viewers. Extensive construction of cable systems began during the 1980s to provide service to people in all geographic regions. In the 1990s, many cable television companies started to use fiber optics for new systems and to upgrade existing systems. Fiber optic technology increases network capacity, thus allowing more channels to subscribers, and allows for higher-quality sound reception.

Today, both cable television and telephone companies are using advanced technologies to modernize their equipment and build new telecommunications systems that allow voice, data, and video transmissions over the same lines. Telephone companies are building networks of cables and other equipment that will allow them to offer cable services, and cable television companies are entering the telephone business. Cox Communications and Cablevision Systems are examples of major cable operators offering phone, Internet, and cable service to homes and businesses in many markets. This is expected to generate increased construction activity during the 21st century; however, it is uncertain how many jobs will be generated from the expected boom, as much of the new equipment is maintenance-free and requires far fewer workers in terms of repairs and upkeep.

THE JOB

In the installation of new telephone and electric power lines, workers use power-driven machinery to first dig holes and erect the poles or towers that are used to support the cables. (In some areas, lines must be buried underground, and in these cases installers use power-driven equipment to dig and to place the cables in underground conduits.) These line installers, also called *outside plant technicians* and *construction line workers*, climb the poles using metal rungs (or they use truck-mounted work platforms) and install the necessary equipment and cables.

Installers who work with telephone lines usually leave the ends of the wires free for cable splicers to connect afterward; installers who work with electric power lines usually do the splicing of the wires themselves.

In addition to working with lines for electric power and telephones, installers set up lines for cable television transmission. Such lines carry broadcast signals from microwave towers to customer bases. Cable television lines are hung on the same poles with power and phone lines, or they are buried underground. In some cases, installers must attach other wires to the customer's premises in order to connect the outside lines to indoor television sets.

After line installers have completed the installation of underground conduits or poles, wires, and cables, cable splicers complete the line connections; they also rearrange wires when lines are changed. To join the individual wires within the cable, splicers must cut the lead sheath and insulation from the cables. They then test or phase out each conductor to identify corresponding conductors in adjoining cable sections according to electrical diagrams and specifications. At each splice, they either wrap insulation around the wires and seal the joint with a lead sleeve or cover the splice with some other type of closure. Sometimes they fill the sheathing with pressurized air so that leaks can be located and repaired.

In the past, copper was the material of choice for cables, but fiber optics are now replacing the outdated material. Fiber optic cables are hair-thin strands of glass that transmit signals more efficiently than do copper wires. For work with fiber optic cable, splicing is performed in workshop vans located near the splice area. Splicers of copper cables do their work on aerial platforms, down in manholes, in basements, or in underground vaults where the cables are located.

Preventive maintenance and repair work occupy major portions of the line installer's and cable splicer's time. When wires or cables break or poles are knocked down, workers are sent immediately to make emergency repairs. Such repair work is usually necessary after the occurrence of such disasters as storms and earthquakes. The line crew supervisor is notified when there is a break in a line and is directed to the trouble spot by workers who keep a check on the condition of all lines in given areas. During the course of routine periodic inspection, the line installer also makes minor repairs and line changes. Workers often use electric and gas pressure tests to detect possible trouble.

To allow for the demands of high-speed, high-definition transmissions, many telecommunications companies are installing fiber optic cables. The use of hybrid fiber/coax systems requires far less maintenance than traditional copper-based networks. Line installers and cable splicers will spend significantly less time repairing broken wires and cables once hybrid fiber/coax systems become more prevalent. As the cost of fiber cables decrease and become more in line with the costs of copper cables, more cable companies will make the switch.

Included in this occupation are many specialists, such as the following: section line maintainers, tower line repairers, line construction checkers, tower erectors, and cable testers. Other types of related workers include troubleshooters, test desk trouble locators, steel-post installers, radio interference investigators, and electric powerline examiners.

REQUIREMENTS

High School

You'll need math courses to prepare for the technical nature of this career. While in high school you should also take any shop classes that will teach you the principles of electricity and how to work with it. In addition, you will benefit from taking any classes that deal with electricity at a vocational or technical college in your area. Other high school shop classes, such as machinery, will give you the opportunity to work with tools and improve your hand-eye coordination. Science classes that involve lab work will also be beneficial. Take computer classes so that you will be able to use this tool in your professional life. Because you may be frequently interacting with customers, take English, speech, and other courses that will help you develop communication skills.

Postsecondary Training

Many companies prefer to hire applicants with a high school diploma or the equivalent. Although specific educational courses are not required, you'll need certain qualifications. It is helpful to have some knowledge of the basic principles of electricity and the procedures involved in line installation; such information can be obtained through attending technical programs or having been a member of the armed forces. Many employers, particularly for cable television installation, prefer to hire applicants who have received some technical training or completed a trade school or technical program that offers certification classes in technology such as fiber optics. Training can also be obtained through special classes offered through trade associations. The Society of Cable Telecommunications Engineers (SCTE) offers seminars that provide hands-on, technical training.

In many companies, entry-level employees must complete a formal apprenticeship program combining classroom instruction with

Work in this field often involves climbing poles and ladders, so you'll need to feel comfortable with heights. *(David R. Frazier, The Image Works)*

supervised on-the-job training. These programs often last several years and are administered by both the employer and the union representing the employees. The programs may involve computer-assisted instruction as well as hands-on experience with simulated environments.

Certification or Licensing

Though not a requirement for employment, certification demonstrates to employers that a line installer has achieved a certain level of technical training and has been proven qualified to perform certain functions. The SCTE offers several certification designations to applicants who show technical knowledge and practical skills by passing both multiple-choice and essay-based examinations. (Contact information for the SCTE is listed at the end of this article.)

Employers may also give preemployment tests to applicants to determine verbal, mechanical, and mathematical aptitudes; some employers test applicants for such physical qualifications as stamina, balance, coordination, and strength. Workers who drive a company vehicle need a driver's license and a good driving record.

Unions represent many workers, and union membership may be required as a condition for employment. Two unions that represent many line installers and cable splicers are the International Brotherhood of Electrical Workers (IBEW) and the Communications Workers of America (CWA).

Other Requirements

You'll need manual dexterity and to be in good physical shape. Much of your work will involve climbing poles and ladders, so you'll need to feel comfortable with heights. You also need to be strong in order to carry heavy equipment up poles and ladders. Also, because lines and cables are color coded, you should have the ability to distinguish such colors. You may have extensive contact with the public and need to be polite and courteous.

EXPLORING

In high school or vocational school, you can test your ability and interest in the occupations of line installer and cable splicer through courses in mathematics, electrical applications, and machine shop. To observe line installers and cable splicers at work, it may be possible to have a school counselor arrange a field trip by calling the public relations office of the local telecommunications company.

Direct training and experience in telephone work may be gained in the armed forces. Frequently, those who have received such training are given preference for job openings and may be hired in positions above the entry level.

EMPLOYERS

There are approximately 275,000 line installers and cable splicers working in the United States. About 59 percent work in the telecommunications industry. Most work for telephone or cable television companies. They also find work with electric power companies. Some installers also work for the freelance construction companies that contract with telecommunications companies.

STARTING OUT

Those who meet the basic requirements and are interested in becoming either a line installer or a cable splicer may inquire about job openings by directly contacting the personnel offices of local telephone companies, utility companies, and cable television providers.

Those enrolled in a trade school or technical institute may be able to find out about job openings through their schools' career services office. Occasionally, employers will contact teachers and program administrators, so it is helpful to check with them also. Some positions are advertised through classified advertisements in the newspaper. Because many line installers are members of unions such as the CWA and the IBEW, job seekers can contact their local offices for job leads and assistance or visit these unions' Web sites.

ADVANCEMENT

Entry-level line installers are generally hired as helpers, trainees, or ground workers; cable splicers tend to work their way up from the position of line installer.

After successfully completing an on-the-job training program, the employee will be assigned either as a line crew member under the guidance of a line supervisor or as a cable splicer's helper under the guidance of experienced splicers. Cable splicers' helpers advance to positions of qualified cable splicers after three to four years of working experience.

Both the line installer and the cable splicer must continue to receive training throughout their careers, not only to qualify for advancement but also to keep up with the technological changes that occur in the industry. Usually it takes line installers about six years to reach top pay for their job; top pay for cable splicers is earned after about five to seven years of work experience.

In companies represented by unions, opportunities for advancement may be based on seniority. Workers who demonstrate technical expertise in addition to certain personal characteristics, such as good judgment, planning skills, and the ability to deal with people, may progress to foremen or line crew supervisors. With additional training, the line installer or the cable splicer may advance to telephone installer, telephone repairer, communications equipment technician, or another higher ranked position.

EARNINGS

For line installers and cable splicers, earnings vary according to different regions of the country, and as with most occupations, work experience and length of service determine advances in scale. The U.S. Department of Labor reports the following median annual earnings for telecommunications line installers and repairers by employer in 2006: wired telecommunications carriers, $55,620; telecommunications resellers, $54,420; cable and other subscription programming, $39,720; and cable and other program distribution, $38,800. Salaries for all line installers and repairers ranged from less than $24,700 to $68,220 or more per year. When emergencies arise and overtime is necessary during unscheduled hours, workers are guaranteed a minimum rate of pay that is higher than their regular rate.

Beginning workers and those with only a few years of experience make significantly less than more experienced workers. As mentioned earlier, the turnover rate in these occupations is low; therefore, many workers are in the higher wage categories. Also, cable splicers who work with fiber optics tend to earn more than those who work with copper cables.

Telecommunications companies often provide workers with many benefits. Although benefits vary from company to company, in general, most workers receive paid holidays, vacations, and sick leaves. In addition, most companies offer medical, dental, and life insurance plans. Some companies offer pension plans.

WORK ENVIRONMENT

Most line installers and cable splicers work standard 40-hour weeks, though evening and weekend work is not unusual. For example, line installers and cable splicers who work for construction companies may need to schedule their work around contractors' activities and then be required to rush to complete a job on schedule. Shift work, such as four 10-hour days or working Tuesday through Saturday, is common for many workers. Most workers earn extra pay for any work over 40 hours a week.

Some workers are on call 24 hours a day and need to be available for emergencies. Both occupations require that workers perform their jobs outdoors, often in severe weather conditions when emergency repairs are needed.

There is a great deal of climbing involved in these occupations, and some underground work must be done in stooped and cramped conditions. Cable splicers sometimes perform their work on board a marine craft if they are employed with an underwater cable crew.

The work can be physically demanding and poses significant risk of injury from shocks (for workers who install electric power lines) or falls. The hazards of this work have been greatly reduced, though, by concerted efforts to establish safety standards. Such efforts have been put forward by the telecommunications companies, utility companies, and appropriate labor unions.

OUTLOOK

The U.S. Department of Labor anticipates that employment for line installers and cable splicers will grow more slowly than the average for all occupations through 2016, though the trend will vary among industries. For example, average employment growth is expected for those working specifically for electric companies, while those working as telephone or cable television installers are predicted to have slower-than-average job opportunities due to the growing popularity of wireless and satellite telecommunications technology. There tends to be a low rate of employee turnover, but new employees will be needed to replace those who retire or leave the field.

FOR MORE INFORMATION

For information about union representation, contact
Communications Workers of America
501 Third Street, NW
Washington, DC 20001-2797
Tel: 202-434-1100
http://www.cwa-union.org

International Brotherhood of Electrical Workers
900 Seventh Street, NW
Washington, DC 20001-3886
Tel: 202-833-7000
http://www.ibew.org

For information on careers and the cable industry, contact
National Cable and Telecommunications Association
25 Massachusetts Avenue, NW, Suite 100
Washington, DC 20001-1434
Tel: 202-222-2300
http://www.ncta.com

For information on training seminars and certification, contact
Society of Cable Telecommunications Engineers
140 Philips Road
Exton, PA 19341-1318
Tel: 800-542-5040
Email: scte@scte.org
http://www.scte.org

For information about conferences, special programs, and membership, contact
Women in Cable Telecommunications
14555 Avion Parkway, Suite 250
Chantilly, VA 20151-1117
Tel: 703-234-9810
http://www.wict.org

Marketing Research Analysts

QUICK FACTS

School Subjects
Business
Mathematics

Personal Skills
Following instructions
Technical/scientific

Work Environment
Primarily indoors
Primarily one location

Minimum Education Level
Bachelor's degree

Salary Range
$32,250 to $74,350 to
$112,510+

Certification or Licensing
None available

Outlook
More slowly than the average

DOT
050

GOE
13.02.04

NOC
N/A

O*NET-SOC
19-3021.00

OVERVIEW

Marketing research analysts collect, analyze, and interpret data in order to determine potential demand for a product or service. By examining the buying habits, wants, needs, and preferences of consumers, research analysts are able to recommend ways to improve products and services, increase sales, and expand customer bases. There are approximately 6,000 marketing research analysts employed in the U.S. telecommunications industry.

HISTORY

Knowing what customers want and what prices they are willing to pay have always been concerns of manufacturers and producers of goods and services. As industries have grown and competition for consumers of manufactured goods and services has increased, businesses have turned to marketing research as a way to measure public opinion and assess customer preferences.

Marketing research formally emerged in Germany in the 1920s and in Sweden and France in the 1930s. In the United States, emphasis on marketing research began after World War II. With a desire to study potential markets and gain new customers, U.S. firms hired marketing research specialists, professionals who were able to use statistics and refine research techniques to help companies reach their marketing goals. By the 1980s, research analysts could be found even in a variety of Communist countries, where the quantity of consumer goods being produced was rapidly increasing.

Today, marketing research analysts are employed in many industries including the telecommunications industry. The marketing research analyst is a vital part of the marketing team. By conducting studies and analyzing data, research professionals help telecommunications companies address specific marketing issues and concerns.

THE JOB

Marketing researchers in the telecommunications industry collect and analyze all kinds of information in order to help companies improve their products and services, establish or modify sales and distribution policies, and make decisions regarding future plans and directions. In addition, research analysts are responsible for monitoring both in-house studies and off-site research, interpreting results, providing explanations of compiled data, and developing research tools.

One area of marketing research focuses on company products and services such as cell phones or cable television subscriptions. In order to determine consumer preferences, research analysts collect data on brand names, trademarks, product design, and packaging for existing products, items being test-marketed, and those in experimental stages. Analysts also study competing products and services that are already on the market to help managers and strategic planners develop new products and create appropriate advertising campaigns.

In the sales methods and policy area of marketing research, analysts examine firms' sales records and conduct a variety of sales-related studies. For example, information on sales in various geographical areas is analyzed and compared to previous sales figures, changes in population, and total and seasonal sales volume. By analyzing this data, marketing researchers can identify peak sales periods and recommend ways to target new customers. Such information helps marketers plan future sales campaigns and establish sales quotas and commissions.

Advertising research is closely related to sales research. Studies on the effectiveness of advertising in different parts of the country (for example, a mailing in the Midwest that advertises services provided by Comcast) are conducted and compared to sales records. This research is helpful in planning future advertising campaigns and in selecting the appropriate media to use. If the mailing fails to generate an increase in sales, for example, then the company might try to reach potential customers via a television ad campaign the next time it seeks to advertise its products.

Marketing research that focuses on consumer demand and preferences solicits opinions of the people who use the products or services being considered. In addition to actually conducting opinion studies, marketing researchers often design the ways to obtain the information. They write scripts for telephone interviews, develop direct-mail questionnaires and field surveys, and design focus group programs.

Through one or a combination of these studies, market researchers are able to gather information on consumer reaction to the need for and style, design, price, and use of a product (for example, a new cell phone model). The studies attempt to reveal who uses various products or services, identify potential customers, or get suggestions for product or service improvement. This information is helpful for forecasting sales, planning design modifications, and determining changes in features.

Once information has been gathered, marketing researchers analyze the findings. They then detail their findings and recommendations in a written report and often orally present them to management as well.

A number of professionals compose the marketing research team. The *project supervisor* is responsible for overseeing a study from beginning to end. The *statistician* determines the sample size—or the number of people to be surveyed—and compares the number of responses. The project supervisor or statistician, in conjunction with other specialists (such as *demographers* and *psychologists*), often determines the number of interviews to be conducted as well as their locations. *Field interviewers* survey people in various public places, such as shopping malls, office complexes, and popular attractions. *Telemarketers* gather information by placing calls to current or potential customers, to people listed in telephone books, or to those who appear on specialized lists obtained from list houses. Once questionnaires come in from the field, *tabulators* and *coders* examine the data, count the answers, code noncategorical answers, and tally the primary counts. The marketing research analyst then analyzes the returns, writes up the final report, and makes recommendations to the client or to management.

Marketing research analysts must be thoroughly familiar with research techniques and procedures. Sometimes the research problem is clearly defined, and information can be gathered readily. Other times, company executives may know only that a problem exists as evidenced by a decline in sales. In these cases, the marketing research analyst is expected to collect the facts that will aid in revealing and resolving the problem.

The Most Admired
Telecommunications Companies, 2008

Each year, *Fortune* magazine asks executives, directors, and securities analysts to select the companies in their own industry that they admire the most. Here are the five most admired telecommunications companies:

1. AT&T (http://www.att.com)

2. Verizon Communications (http://www22.verizon.com)

3. Comcast (http://www.comcast.com)

4. Virgin Media (http://www.virgin.com/Companies/VirginMedia/VirginMedia.aspx)

5. DirecTV Group (http://www.directv.com)

Source: *Fortune*

REQUIREMENTS

High School

Most employers require their marketing research analysts to hold at least a bachelor's degree, so a college preparatory program is advised. Classes in English, marketing, economics, mathematics, psychology, and sociology are particularly important. Courses in computing are especially useful, since a great deal of tabulation and statistical analysis is required in the marketing research field.

Postsecondary Training

A bachelor's degree is essential for careers in marketing research. Majors in marketing, business administration, statistics, computer science, history, or economics provide a good background for most types of research positions. In addition, course work in sociology and psychology is helpful for those who are leaning toward consumer demand and opinion research. Since quantitative skills are important in various types of industrial or analytic research, students interested in these areas should take statistics, econometrics, survey design, sampling theory, and other mathematics courses.

Many employers prefer that a marketing research analyst hold a master's degree as well as a bachelor's degree. A master's of business administration, for example, is frequently required on projects calling for complex statistical and business analysis. Graduate work at the doctorate level is not necessary for most positions, but it is highly desirable for those who plan to become involved in advanced research studies.

Certification and Licensing
The Marketing Research Association offers certification for marketing research analysts. Contact the association for more information.

Other Requirements
To work in this career, you should be intelligent, detail oriented, and accurate; have the ability to work easily with words and numbers; and be particularly interested in solving problems through data collection and analysis. In addition, you must be patient and persistent, since long hours are often required when working on complex studies.

As part of the market research team, you must be able to work well with others and have an interest in people. The ability to communicate, both orally and in writing, is also important, since you will be responsible for writing up detailed reports on the findings in various studies and presenting recommendations to management.

EXPLORING

You can find many opportunities in high school to learn more about the necessary skills for the field of marketing research. For example, experiments in science, problems in student government, committee work, and other school activities provide exposure to situations similar to those encountered by marketing research analysts.

You can also seek part-time employment as a survey interviewer at local marketing research firms. Gathering field data for consumer surveys offers valuable experience through actual contact with both the public and marketing research supervisors. In addition, many companies seek a variety of other employees to code, tabulate, and edit surveys; monitor telephone interviews; and validate the information entered on written questionnaires. You can search for job listings in local newspapers and on the Web or apply directly to research organizations.

If you are interested in working in the telecommunications industry, it is a good idea to learn as much as you can about cable providers, wireless and traditional phone companies, and other service providers. Study their marketing materials on television, radio, the Internet, and in the U.S. mail to learn more about the products and services they offer. Try to determine which company has the best advertising campaign and identify the reasons why you believe that company has a superior campaign. Write your own marketing materials for companies that did not impress you.

EMPLOYERS

Approximately 6,000 marketing research analysts are employed in the U.S. telecommunications industry. Large corporations including those that specialize in telecommunications, industrial firms, advertising agencies, data collection businesses, and private research organizations that handle local surveys for companies on a contract basis employ marketing research analysts. While many marketing research organizations offer a broad range of services, some firms subcontract parts of an overall project out to specialized companies. For example, one research firm may concentrate on product interviews, while another might focus on measuring the effectiveness of product advertising.

Although many smaller firms located all across the country outsource studies to marketing research firms, these research firms, along with most large corporations that employ marketing research analysts, are located in such big cities as New York or Chicago. Approximately 90 percent of salaried marketing research analysts are employed in private industry, but opportunities also exist in government and academia, as well as at hospitals, public libraries, and a variety of other types of organizations.

STARTING OUT

Students with a graduate degree in marketing research and experience in quantitative techniques have the best chances of landing jobs as marketing research analysts. Since a bachelor's degree in marketing or business is usually not sufficient to obtain such a position, many employees without postgraduate degrees start out as research assistants, trainees, interviewers, or questionnaire editors. In such positions, those aspiring to the job of research analyst can gain valuable experience conducting interviews, analyzing data, and writing reports.

Use your college career services office, the Web, and help wanted sections of local newspapers to look for job leads. Another way to get into the marketing research field is through personal and professional contacts. Names and telephone numbers of potential employers may come from professors, friends, or relatives. Students who have participated in internships or have held marketing research-related jobs on a part-time basis while in school or during the summer may be able to obtain employment at these firms or at similar organizations. Finally, CTAM: Cable & Telecommunications Association for Marketing offers job listings at its Web site, http://www.ctam.com.

ADVANCEMENT

Most marketing research professionals begin as *junior analysts* or *research assistants*. In these positions, they help in preparing questionnaires and related materials, training survey interviewers, and tabulating and coding survey results. After gaining sufficient experience in these and other aspects of research project development, employees are often assigned their own research projects, which usually involve supervisory and planning responsibilities. A typical promotion path for those climbing the company ladder might be from assistant researcher to marketing research analyst to assistant manager and then to manager of a branch office for a large private research firm. From there, some professionals become market research executives or research directors for industrial or business firms.

Since marketing research analysts learn about all aspects of marketing on the job, some advance by moving to positions in other departments, such as advertising or sales. Depending on the interests and experience of marketing professionals, other areas of employment to which they can advance include data processing, teaching at the university level, statistics, economics, and industrial research and development.

In general, few employees go from starting positions to executive jobs at one company. Advancement often requires changing employers. Therefore, marketing research analysts who want to move up the ranks frequently go from one company to another, sometimes many times during their careers.

EARNINGS

Beginning salaries in marketing research depend on the qualifications of the employee, the nature of the position, and the size of the firm. Interviewers, coders, tabulators, editors, and a variety of other employees usually get paid by the hour and may start at $6 or more per hour. The U.S. Department of Labor reported that in 2006, mean annual earnings of marketing research analysts employed in the telecommunications industry were $74,350. Salaries for marketing research analysts employed in all fields ranged from less than $32,250 to more than $112,510. Experienced analysts working in supervisory positions at large firms can earn even higher earnings. Market research directors earn up to $200,000.

Because business or industrial firms employ most marketing research workers, they receive typical fringe benefit packages, including health and life insurance, pension plans, and paid vacation and sick leave.

WORK ENVIRONMENT

Marketing research analysts usually work a 40-hour week. Occasionally, overtime is necessary in order to meet project deadlines. Although they frequently interact with a variety of marketing research team members, analysts also do a lot of independent work, analyzing data, writing reports, and preparing statistical charts.

While most marketing research analysts work in offices located at the firm's main headquarters, those who supervise interviewers may go into the field to oversee work. In order to attend conferences, meet with clients, or check on the progress of various research studies, many marketing research analysts find that regular travel is required.

OUTLOOK

Despite the fact that the U.S. Department of Labor predicts slower-than-average growth for marketing research analysts employed in the telecommunications industry, opportunities should still be good since telecommunications companies are constantly looking for ways to gain the competitive edge and attract more customers. While many new graduates are attracted to the field, those individuals who hold a master's degree or doctorate in marketing research, statistics, economics, or computer science will be in a superior position to obtain the most attractive jobs and the highest salaries in this occupational employment market.

The U.S. Department of Labor predicts that employment for marketing research analysts employed in all industries will grow faster than the average for all occupations through 2016. Increasing competition among producers of consumer goods and services and industrial products, combined with a growing awareness of the value of marketing research data, will contribute to opportunities in the field. Opportunities will be best for those with graduate degrees.

FOR MORE INFORMATION

For information on college chapters, internship opportunities, and financial aid opportunities, contact
American Advertising Federation
1101 Vermont Avenue, NW, Suite 500
Washington, DC 20005-6306
Tel: 202-898-0089
Email: aaf@aaf.org
http://www.aaf.org

For information on graduate programs, contact
American Association for Public Opinion Research
PO Box 14263
Lenexa, KS 66285-4263
Tel: 913-895-4601
Email: info@aapor.org
http://www.aapor.org

For information on advertising agencies, contact
American Association of Advertising Agencies
405 Lexington Avenue, 18th Floor
New York, NY 10174-1801
Tel: 212-682-2500
http://www.aaaa.org

For career resources and job listings, contact
American Marketing Association
311 South Wacker Drive, Suite 5800
Chicago, IL 60606-6629
Tel: 800-262-1150
http://www.marketingpower.com

For industry information, contact
CTAM: Cable & Telecommunications Association for Marketing

201 North Union Street, Suite 440
Alexandria, VA 22314-2642
Tel: 703-549-4200
Email: info@ctam.com
http://www.ctam.com

For comprehensive information on market and opinion research, contact
Council for Marketing and Opinion Research
110 National Drive, 2nd Floor
Glastonbury, CT 06033-1212
Tel: 860-657-1881
Email: information@cmor.org
http://www.cmor.org

For information on graduate programs in marketing, contact
Council of American Survey Research Organizations
170 North Country Road, Suite 4
Port Jefferson, NY 11777-2606
Tel: 631-928-6954
Email: casro@casro.org
http://www.casro.org

For information on education, training, and certification, contact
Marketing Research Association
110 National Drive, 2nd Floor
Glastonbury, CT 06033-1212
Tel: 860-682-1000
Email: email@mra-net.org
http://www.mra-net.org

For information on careers and the cable industry, contact
National Cable & Telecommunications Association
25 Massachusetts Avenue, NW, Suite 100
Washington, DC 20001-1434
Tel: 202-222-2300
http://www.ncta.com

For information on educational programs and job opportunities in wireless technology (cellular, PCS, and satellite), contact
Personal Communications Industry Association
901 North Washington Street, Suite 600

Alexandria VA 22314-1535
Tel: 800-759-0300
http://www.pcia.com

For career information, visit
Careers Outside the Box: Survey Research: A Fun, Exciting,
    Rewarding Career
http://www.casro.org/careers

Microelectronics Technicians

OVERVIEW

Microelectronics technicians work in research laboratories assisting the engineering staff to develop and construct prototype and custom-designed microchips. Microchips, often called simply chips, are tiny but extremely complex electronic devices that control the operations of many kinds of communications equipment, consumer products, industrial controls, aerospace guidance systems, and medical electronics. The process of manufacturing chips is often called fabrication. Microelectronics technicians are often classified under the career category, electrical and electronics engineering technician. About 13,000 people work as electrical and electronics engineering technicians in the telecommunications industry.

HISTORY

The science of electronics is only about 100 years old. Yet electronics has had an enormous impact on the way people live. Without electronics, things like television, telephones, computers, X-ray machines, and radar would not be possible. Today, nearly every area of industry, manufacturing, entertainment, health care, and communications uses electronics to improve the quality of people's lives. This article you are reading, for example, was created by people using electronic equipment, from the writing of each article to the design, layout, and production of the book itself.

The earliest electronic systems depended on electron vacuum tubes to conduct current. But these devices were too bulky and too

slow for many of their desired tasks. In the early 1950s, the introduction of microelectronics—that is, the design and production of
integrated circuits and products using integrated circuits—allowed
engineers and scientists to design faster and faster and smaller and
smaller electronic devices. Initially developed for military equipment
and space technology, integrated circuits have made possible such
everyday products as personal computers, microwave ovens, and
digital video disc players and are found in nearly every electronic
product that people use today.

Integrated circuits are miniaturized electronic systems. Integrated
circuits include many interconnected electronic components such as
transistors, capacitors, and resistors, produced on or in a single thin
slice of a semiconductor material. Semiconductors are so named
because they are substances with electrical properties somewhere
between those of conductors and insulators. The semiconductor
used most frequently in microchips is silicon, so microchips are also
sometimes called silicon chips. Often smaller than a fingernail, chips
may contain multiple layers of complex circuitry stacked on top of
each other. The word integrated refers to the way the circuitry is
blended into the chip during the fabrication process.

The reliance on electronic technology has created a need for
skilled personnel to design, construct, test, and repair electronic
components and products including those used to create telecommunications products, equipment, and infrastructure. The growing
uses of microelectronics have created a corresponding demand for
technicians specially trained to assist in the design and development
of new applications of electronic technology.

THE JOB

Microelectronics technicians typically assist in the development of prototypes, or new kinds, of electronic components and products. They
work closely with electronics engineers, who design the components,
build and test them, and prepare the component or product for large-
scale manufacture. Such components usually require the integrated
operation of several or many different types of chips.

Microelectronics technicians generally work from a schematic
received from the design engineer. The schematic contains a list of
the parts that will be needed to construct the component and the
layout that the technician will follow. The technician gathers the
parts and prepares the materials to be used. Following the schematic,
the technician constructs the component and then uses a variety of
sophisticated, highly sensitive equipment to test the component's

performance. One such test measures the component's burn-in time. During this test the component is kept in continuous operation for a long period of time, and the component and its various features are subjected to a variety of tests to be certain the component will stand up to extended use.

If the component fails to function according to its required specifications, the microelectronics technician must be able to troubleshoot the design, locating where the component has failed, and replace one part for a new or different part. Test results are reported to the engineering staff, and the technician may be required to help evaluate the results and prepare reports based on these evaluations. In many situations, the microelectronics technician will work closely with the engineer to solve any problems arising in the component's operation and design.

After the testing period, the microelectronics technician is often responsible for assisting in the technical writing of the component's specifications. These specifications are used for integrating the component into new or redesigned products or for developing the process for the component's large-scale manufacture. The microelectronics technician helps to develop the production system for the component and will also write reports on the component's functions, uses, and performance.

"You really need to have good communication skills," says Kyle Turner, a microelectronics technician at White Oak Semiconductor in Virginia. "Not only do you have to let others know what you mean and explain yourself, you often have to train new employees in the specifics of your product."

Microelectronics technicians perform many of the same functions as electronics technicians, but generally work only in the development laboratory. More experienced technicians may assume greater responsibilities. They work closely with the engineering staff to develop layout and assembly procedures and to use their own knowledge of microelectronics to suggest changes in circuitry or installation. Often they are depended upon to simplify the assembly or maintenance requirements. After making any changes, they test the performance of the component, analyze the results, and suggest and perform further modifications to the component's design. Technicians may fabricate new parts using various machine tools, supervise the installation of the new component, or become involved in training and supervising other technical personnel.

Some microelectronics technicians specialize in the fabrication and testing of semiconductors and integrated circuits. These technicians are usually called *semiconductor development technicians*.

They are involved in the development of prototype chips, following the direction of engineering staff, and perform the various steps required for making and testing new integrated circuits.

REQUIREMENTS

The advanced technology involved in microelectronics means that post-high school education or training is a requirement for entering the field. You should consider enrolling in a two-year training program at a community college or vocational training facility and expect to earn a certificate or an associate's degree. Like most microelectronics technicians, Kyle Turner completed a two-year degree in electronics as well as an extensive on-the-job training program.

High School

High school students interested in microelectronics can begin their preparation by taking courses such as algebra and geometry. If you have taken science courses, especially chemistry and physics, you will have a better chance to enter an apprenticeship program and you will be more prepared for postsecondary educational programs.

"Math skills are really important," says Turner. "You have to be able to take accurate measurements and make good calculations."

Knowledge of proper grammar and spelling is necessary for writing reports, and you should also develop your reading comprehension. Taking industrial classes, such as metalworking, wood shop, auto shop, and machine shop, and similar courses in plastics, electronics, and construction techniques will be helpful. Another area of study is computer science, and you would enhance your postsecondary educational opportunities if you obtained experience in computer technology.

Postsecondary Training

Few employers will hire people for microelectronics technician positions who do not have advanced training. Although some low-skilled workers may advance into technician jobs, employers generally prefer to hire people with higher education. Technician and associate's degree programs are available at many community colleges and at public and private vocational training centers and schools. Many technical schools are located where the microelectronics industry is particularly active. These schools often have programs tailored specifically for the needs of companies in their area. Community colleges offer a greater degree of flexibility in that they are able to keep up with the rapid advances and changes in technology and can redesign their courses and programs to meet the new requirements. You can expect to study in such areas as mathematics, including algebra, geometry, and calculus; physics; and electronics engineering technology. Many schools will require you to take courses in English composition, as well as fulfill other course requirements in the humanities and social sciences.

Other methods of entry are three- and four-year apprenticeship programs. These programs generally involve on-the-job training by the employer. You can locate apprenticeship opportunities through your high school guidance office, in listings in local newspapers, or by contacting local manufacturers.

Military service is also an excellent method for beginning an electronics career. The military is one of the largest users of electronics technology and offers training and educational programs to enlisted personnel in many areas of electronics.

Finally, the rapid advancements in microelectronics may make it desirable or even necessary for you to continue to take courses, receive training, and study various trade journals throughout your career.

Certification or Licensing

Certification is not mandatory in most areas of electronics (although technicians working with radio-transmitting devices are required to be licensed by the Federal Communications Commission), but voluntary certification may prove useful in locating work and in increasing your pay and responsibilities. The International Society of Certified Electronics Technicians (ISCET) offers certification testing to technicians with four years of experience or schooling, as well as associate-level testing of basic electronics for beginning technicians. ISCET also offers a variety of study and training materials to help you prepare for the certification tests.

Other Requirements

Microelectronics technicians are involved in creating prototypes—that is, new and untested technology. This aspect of the field brings special responsibilities for carrying out assembly and testing procedures: These must be performed with a high degree of precision. When assembling a new component, for example, you must be able to follow the design engineer's specifications and instructions exactly. Similar diligence and attention to detail are necessary when following the different procedures for testing the new components. An understanding of the underlying technology is important.

A microelectronics technician at an Ericsson mobile phone factory uses a microscope to check mobile phone circuits. *(Alex Farnsworth, The Image Works)*

EXPLORING

You can begin exploring this field by getting involved in science clubs and working on electronics projects at home. Any part-time experience repairing electronic equipment will give you exposure to the basics of electronics.

You can find many resources for electronics experiments and projects in your school or local library or on the Internet. Summer employment in any type of electronics will be useful. Talking with someone who works in the field may help you narrow your focus to one particular area of electronics.

If you are interested in working in telecommunications, you should read as many books and magazines as you can about the field. You can also visit the Web sites of professional associations and ask your guidance counselor to help arrange an information interview with a microelectronics technician who works in the industry.

EMPLOYERS

About 13,000 people work as electrical and electronics engineering technicians in the telecommunications industry. Others work in the computer and electronics industries. Some microelectronics technicians are self-employed, some work for large corporations, and others work in government-related jobs.

STARTING OUT

Most schools provide job placement services to students completing their degree program. Many offer on-the-job training as a part of the program. An internship or other real-life experience is desirable but not necessary. Many companies have extensive on-site training programs.

Newspapers and trade journals are full of openings for people working in electronics, and some companies recruit new hires directly on campus. Government employment offices are also good sources when looking for job leads.

ADVANCEMENT

Microelectronics technicians who choose to continue their education can expect to increase their responsibilities and be eligible to advance to supervisory and managerial positions.

Microelectronics Are Used In . . .

- Cellular Phones
- Personal Digital Assistants
- Televisions
- Radios
- Computers
- Compact Disc Players
- Digital Video Disc Players
- Computer and Video Games
- GPS Devices
- Microwave Ovens
- Radar
- X Rays
- Robotics
- Space and Weapons Technology

Microelectronics technicians may also desire to enter other, more demanding areas of microelectronics such as semiconductor development and engineering. Additional education may be necessary; engineers will be required to hold at least a four-year degree in electronics engineering.

Earning certification from the International Society of Certified Electronics Technicians may be part of the requirement for advancement in certain companies.

EARNINGS

According to the U.S. Department of Labor, median annual earnings of electrical and electronics engineering technicians employed by wired telecommunications carriers were $54,890 in 2006. Salaries for all electrical and electronics engineering technicians ranged from less than $30,120 to more than $73,200. Those in managerial or supervisory positions earn higher salaries, ranging between $55,000 and $85,000 per year. Wage rates vary greatly, according to skill level, type of employer, and location. Most employers offer some fringe benefits including paid holidays and vacations, sick leave, and life and health insurance.

WORK ENVIRONMENT

Microelectronics technicians generally work a 40-hour week, although they may be assigned to different shifts or be required to work weekends and holidays. Overtime and holiday pay can usually be expected in such circumstances. The work setting is extremely clean, well lighted, and dust free.

Microelectronics technicians have many duties, and this requires them to be flexible yet focused as they perform their duties. They have to be exact and precise in their work no matter what they're doing, whether building an electronic component, running the tests, or recording the data. The fact that each day is often very different from the one before it is an aspect of the job that many technicians find appealing.

"One of the best things about the job is that it's always changing. We're always trying to make a better product, reduce cycle time, make it smaller or cheaper," says Turner. "You're always learning because it changes like crazy."

OUTLOOK

Employment for microelectronics technicians in the telecommunications industry is expected to decline through 2016. The increasing reliability and durability of electronic technology will reduce employment for technicians. Similarly, increasing imports of microelectronics products, components, and technology will cause a decrease in production in this country, which will in turn decrease the numbers of microelectronics technicians needed here. Additionally, the use of advanced technologies, such as computer-aided design and drafting and computer simulation, will improve worker productivity and limit employment growth. Technicians who are certified and who have advanced education will have the best employment prospects. Overall, employment in the electronics industry is also expected to decline.

FOR MORE INFORMATION

For information on certification and student chapters, contact
International Society of Certified Electronics Technicians
3608 Pershing Avenue
Fort Worth, TX 76107-4527
Tel: 800-946-0201
Email: info@iscet.org
http://www.iscet.org

For information on careers and the cable industry, contact
National Cable & Telecommunications Association
25 Massachusetts Avenue, NW, Suite 100
Washington, DC 20001-1434
Tel: 202-222-2300
http://www.ncta.com

For information on educational programs and job opportunities in wireless technology (cellular, PCS, and satellite), contact
Personal Communications Industry Association
901 North Washington Street, Suite 600
Alexandria VA 22314-1535
Tel: 800-759-0300
http://www.pcia.com

For information on careers, educational programs, educational seminars, and distance learning, contact
Society of Cable Telecommunications Engineers
140 Philips Road
Exton, PA 19341-1318
Tel: 800-542-5040

Email: scte@scte.org
http://www.scte.org

For information on semiconductors, a glossary of terms, and industry information, contact
Semiconductor Industry Association
181 Metro Drive, Suite 450
San Jose, CA 95110-1344
Tel: 408-436-6600
Email: mailbox@sia-online.org
http://www.sia-online.org

Optical Engineers

OVERVIEW

Optical engineers apply the concepts of optics to research, design, and develop applications in a broad range of areas. Optics, which involves the properties of light and how it interacts with matter, is a branch of physics and engineering. Optical engineers study the way light is produced, transmitted, detected, and measured to determine ways it can be used and to build devices using optical technology.

HISTORY

The study of the properties of light began during the 1600s when Galileo built telescopes to observe the planets and stars. Scientists, such as Sir Isaac Newton, conducted experiments and studies that contributed to the understanding of light and how it operates. Among Newton's many experiments was his work with prisms that separated sunlight into a spectrum of colors. Christiaan Huygens, a Dutch physicist, also conducted important studies to develop a theory that concerned the wave properties of light.

During the 1800s, other physicists and scientists performed research that confirmed Huygens's theory and advanced the study of light even further. By the mid-1800s, scientists were able to measure the speed of light and had developed means to show how color bands of the light spectrum were created by atoms of chemical elements. In 1864, a British physicist, James C. Maxwell, proposed the electromagnetic theory of light.

Two of the most important discoveries of the 20th century were the development of lasers and fiber optics. The first laser was built by an American physicist, Theodore H. Maiman, in 1960. In 1966, it was discovered that light could travel through glass fibers, which led to the development of fiber optic technology.

Optics, the branch of science that studies the manipulation of light, is a growing field. Engineers today work in applications that include image processing, information processing, wireless communications, electronic technology (including compact disc players, digital video disc players, high-definition televisions, and laser printers), astronomical observation, atomic research, robotics, military surveillance, water-quality monitoring, undersea monitoring, and medical and scientific procedures and instruments.

THE JOB

Optical engineers may work in any of the many subfields or related branches of optics. Three of the largest areas are physical optics, which is concerned with the wave properties of light; quantum optics, which studies photons, or individual particles of light; and geometrical optics, which involves optical instruments used to detect and measure light. Other subfields of optics include integrated optics, nonlinear optics, electron optics, magneto-optics, and space optics.

Optical engineers combine their knowledge of optics with other engineering concepts, such as mechanical engineering, electrical engineering, and computer engineering, to determine applications and build devices using optics technology. Optical engineers design precision optical systems for cameras, telescopes, or lens systems. In designing this equipment, they test that all parts perform as required, diagnose any malfunctioning parts, and correct any defects. Together with electrical and mechanical engineers, they work on the overall design of systems using optical components.

In creating a new product using optical technology, optical engineers go through a multistep engineering process. First, they study the application or problem to understand it thoroughly. Then they brainstorm to come up with possible solutions to the problem. After developing a creative concept, engineers transform it into a design or several designs. They work out all of the details and create a computer-generated model or test unit. This model or unit is tested, and any required revisions to the design are made and tested again. This process continues until the design proves satisfactory. The design is then sent to production, and a product is manufactured. The process is completed with marketing of the product.

For some products, an engineer may perform all of these steps except marketing. Other products require a team of engineers and may include other professionals such as industrial designers, technologists, and technicians.

Some optical engineers specialize in lasers and fiber optics. These engineers, also known as *fiber optics engineers* and *laser and fiber optics engineers*, design, develop, modify, and build equipment and components that utilize laser and fiber optic technology. Lasers are used to produce extremely powerful beams of light that can be transmitted through fiber optics, which are hair-like strands of plastic-coated glass fibers. Using this technology, lasers can cut through material as hard as a diamond, travel over long distances without any loss of power (a quality that is extremely important for applications in the telecommunications industry), and detect extremely small movements. Lasers also can be used to record, store, and transmit information.

These engineers may be involved in testing laser systems or developing applications for lasers in areas such as telecommunications, medicine, defense, manufacturing, and construction.

Fiber optics engineers may specialize and work within a specific area of fiber optic technology. They may work with fiber optic imaging, which involves using fiber optics to transmit light or images. These engineers also use fiber optics to rotate, enlarge, shrink, and enhance images. A second area of specialization involves working with sensors. These engineers work with devices that measure temperature, pressure, force, and other physical features. A third type of specialization is in communications, where fiber optic networks allow voice, data, sound, and images to be transmitted over cables. This is used in telephone systems, computer networks, and undersea fiber optic communications systems.

Optical engineers use many different types of equipment to perform their work. Among them are spectrometers, spectrum analyzers, digital energy meters, calorimeters, laser power meters, leak detectors, and wattmeters.

REQUIREMENTS

High School
While in high school, take physical science, physics, chemistry, geometry, algebra, trigonometry, calculus, social studies, English, composition, and computer science classes. Courses in computer-aided design are also helpful. Honors classes in science and mathematics are recommended.

Postsecondary Training
A bachelor's degree in engineering is required to become an optical engineer. Most engineering programs take four or five years to complete. Many students also receive advanced degrees, such as a

master's of science degree or a doctorate degree, as they are required for higher-level positions.

There are about 120 colleges and universities in the United States and approximately five in Canada that offer classes in optics. Only a very small number of schools, though, offer programs that grant degrees in optical engineering, including the University of Alabama-Huntsville, the University of Arizona, the University of California-Davis, and Rose-Hulman Institute of Technology (all of which are accredited by the Accreditation Board for Engineering Technology). Most colleges offer degrees in a related field, such as electrical engineering or physics, with a specialization in optics.

Because each college program is unique, classes in optical engineering may be offered through various departments, such as physics, electrical and computer engineering, electronic and electrical engineering, electronics and photonics imaging, optical engineering, or optical science. Some schools emphasize the engineering aspects of optics, whereas others focus on optical science or the research aspects of optics. Optical science varies from optical engineering in that it is more concerned with studying the properties of light and its interaction with matter than in developing applications that utilize optical technology.

Classes vary based on the type of program, but they generally include intensive laboratory experience and courses in mathematics, physics, chemistry, electronics, and geometric and wave optics. Advanced courses may include electro-optics, lasers, optical systems design, infrared systems design, quantum mechanics, polarization, fiber optics communication, and optical tests and measurement.

Some colleges require internships or cooperative work programs during which students work at a related job for one to three semesters. Alternating study with work experience is an excellent way to gain on-the-job experience before graduation and can lead to employment opportunities upon graduation.

A high number of students receive Master of Science degrees, which generally take two years of additional study beyond a bachelor's degree. Those who plan to work in research generally earn doctorate degrees, which take four years of additional study beyond a bachelor's degree.

Because the types of programs vary, you should thoroughly research and investigate as many colleges as possible. SPIE—the International Society for Optical Engineering, provides a detailed directory of colleges and universities offering optics courses and describes programs and requirements in depth.

Certification or Licensing

All states require engineers to be licensed. There are two levels of licensing for engineers. Professional engineers (PEs) have graduated from an accredited engineering curriculum, have four years of engineering experience, and have passed a written exam. Engineering graduates need not wait until they have four years experience, however, to start the licensure process. Those who pass the Fundamentals of Engineering examination after graduating are called engineers in training (EITs), engineer interns, or intern engineers. The EIT certification usually is valid for 10 years. After acquiring suitable work experience, EITs can take the second examination, the Principles and Practice of Engineering exam, to gain full PE licensure.

Other Requirements

To become an optical engineer, you need to have a strong foundation in mathematics and physics as well as an inquisitive and analytical mind. You should be good at problem solving, enjoy challenges, and be methodical, precise, and attentive to details. You should be able to work well both individually and with others.

EXPLORING

Students interested in optics can join science and engineering clubs that provide opportunities for experimentation, problem solving, and team building activities. These clubs provide good grounding in science and math principles and the skills students will need as engineers. Ask your science teacher if you can arrange an independent study project. Another way of exploring is through conducting simple experiments on the properties of light. Books on optics often provide instructions for experiments that may be done with a minimum of equipment. Contact your school or local library for books and other resources to explore.

College students may wish to consider joining a student chapter of a professional association such as SPIE or the Optical Society of America. Participation in association events provides an excellent means to meet with professionals working in the area of optical engineering and to learn more about the field. In addition, membership may include a subscription to trade magazines that include interesting and informative articles on optics. Although these associations do charge membership fees, they are relatively inexpensive for college students.

EMPLOYERS

Optical engineers work for companies that produce robotics. They also work in laboratories, hospitals, and universities, as well as in telecommunications and construction. Companies that employ optical engineers can be found in all geographic areas of the country, although some areas have a higher concentration than others. Employers located in areas along the Atlantic coast, from Boston to Washington, D.C., and in large metropolitan areas around cities such as San Jose, Los Angeles, Dallas, Houston, and Orlando provide many opportunities for optical engineers.

STARTING OUT

Some students work part-time or during the summer during their college years as laser technicians, optics technicians, or in another related technician job. This work experience is not only a valuable learning tool, but it may lead to a full-time employment offer once they complete their education.

Students in an undergraduate or graduate program can learn about job openings through internships or cooperative programs in which they have participated. College career services offices can also be a source of job leads. Professional associations also provide information on companies that are seeking optical engineers. In many cases, new graduates research companies that hire optical engineers and apply directly to them.

ADVANCEMENT

Optical engineers with a bachelor's of science degree often start out as assistants to experienced engineers. As they gain experience, they are given more responsibility and independence and move into higher-ranked positions. Engineers who show leadership ability, good communication skills, and management ability may advance to project engineers, project managers, team leaders, or other management positions.

Engineers often return to school to obtain advanced degrees, such as a master's or doctorate degree. With advanced training and experience, they can move into more specialized areas of engineering. Some engineers move into areas of research and become principal engineers or research directors. Engineers may also become college professors or high school teachers.

Some engineers move into sales and marketing. Selling optical devices requires a depth of technical knowledge and the ability to

Books to Read

Chang, Kai (ed.). *Handbook of Optical Components and Engineering.* 2d ed. Hoboken, N.J.: Wiley-Interscience, 2003.

Driggers, Ronald G. *Encyclopedia of Optical Engineering.* Boca Raton, Fla.: CRC Press, 2003.

Kreyszig, Erwin. *Advanced Engineering Mathematics.* 9th ed. Hoboken, N.J.: Wiley, 2005.

Smith, Warren J. *Modern Optical Engineering.* 4th ed. New York: McGraw-Hill Professional, 2007.

Sutherland, Richard L. *Handbook of Nonlinear Optics.* 2d ed. Boca Raton, Fla.: CRC Press, 2003.

explain the features and benefits of a product. Many engineers, after having spent years designing products, are well-equipped for this type of work.

Other optical engineers go into business for themselves, either becoming consulting engineers or starting their own design or manufacturing firms.

EARNINGS

Salaries for optical engineers are similar to those of electrical engineers. According to the U.S. Department of Labor, the median annual earnings of electrical engineers employed in the telecommunications industry were $74,170 in 2006. The lowest paid 10 percent of all electrical engineers earned less than $49,120, and the highest paid 10 percent earned $115,240 or more.

Optics engineers can expect to be paid highly for their expertise, partly due to the fact that the increasing demand for their highly technical skills has outstripped the supply of these highly trained specialized engineers in the employment marketplace. According to a salary survey by Payscale.com, median salaries for optical engineers ranged from $63,000 to $97,000 in 2005.

Companies offer a variety of benefits, including medical, dental, and vision insurance; paid holidays, vacation, sick leave, and personal days; life and disability insurance; pension plans; profit-sharing; 401(k) plans; and tuition assistance programs. Some companies also pay for fees and expenses to participate in professional associations, including travel to national conventions, annual meetings, and trade shows.

WORK ENVIRONMENT

Optical engineers generally work in comfortable surroundings—usually offices or laboratories. Most facilities are equipped with modern equipment and computer workstations. Most engineers work five-day, 40-hour weeks, although overtime is not unusual, particularly when working on a special project. Some companies offer flexible work policies in which engineers can schedule their own hours within certain time periods. Most engineers work with other engineers, technicians, and production personnel.

OUTLOOK

Employment of optical engineers is expected to grow at about as fast as the average through the coming decade. At present, there are more openings for qualified engineers than there are available engineers to fill these positions, so opportunities should be plentiful.

The use of fiber optics in telecommunications is expanding, providing opportunities for engineers in the cable, broadcasting, computer, and telephone industries. New applications are being developed in many other areas, such as the medical and defense fields. The increasing use of automated equipment in manufacturing is also providing opportunities for optical engineers, particularly in applications involving robotics technology.

FOR MORE INFORMATION

To learn about training programs, contact
Fiber Optic Association
1119 South Mission Road, #355
Fallbrook, CA 92028-3225
Tel: 760-451-3655
Email: info@thefoa.org
http://www.thefoa.org

For information on careers and student membership, contact
Lasers and Electro-Optics Society
c/o The Institute of Electrical and Electronics Engineers
445 Hoes Lane
Piscataway, NJ 08854-1331
Tel: 732-562-3892
Email: soc.leo@ieee.org
http://www.ieee.org/leos

For information on careers and the cable industry, contact
National Cable & Telecommunications Association
25 Massachusetts Avenue, NW, Suite 100
Washington, DC 20001-1434
Tel: 202-222-2300
http://www.ncta.com

For information on student membership, contact
Optical Society of America
2010 Massachusetts Avenue, NW
Washington, DC 20036-1012
Tel: 202-223-8130
Email: info@osa.org
http://www.osa.org

For information on educational programs and job opportunities in wireless technology (cellular, PCS, and satellite), contact
Personal Communications Industry Association
901 North Washington Street, Suite 600
Alexandria VA 22314-1535
Tel: 800-759-0300
http://www.pcia.com

For information on careers, educational programs, educational seminars, and distance learning, contact
Society of Cable Telecommunications Engineers
140 Philips Road
Exton, PA 19341-1318
Tel: 800-542-5040
Email: scte@scte.org
http://www.scte.org

For information on colleges, scholarships, student membership, and to participate in an online student forum, visit the SPIE's Web site.
SPIE—The International Society for Optical Engineering
PO Box 10
Bellingham, WA 98227-0010
Tel: 360-676-3290
Email: CustomerService@SPIE.org
http://www.spie.org

For information on optics and careers in the field, visit
Exploring the Science of Light!
http://www.opticsforteens.org

For information on educational programs in optics, visit
**Optics Education: International Directory of Degree Programs
in Optics**
http://www.opticseducation.org

*For job listings and career advice on issues such as networking,
interviewing, and job searching in the field of optics, visit the following Web site organized by the Optical Society of America*
Work in Optics
http://www.workinoptics.com

Technical Writers and Editors

OVERVIEW

Technical writers, sometimes called *technical communicators*, express technical and scientific ideas in easy-to-understand language. *Technical editors* revise written text to correct any errors and make it read smoothly and clearly. They also may coordinate the activities of technical writers, technical illustrators, and other staff in preparing material for publication and oversee the document development and production processes. Technical writers hold about 49,000 jobs in the United States. Only a small percentage of all technical writers work in the telecommunications industry.

HISTORY

Humans have used writing to communicate information for over 5,500 years. Technical writing, though, did not emerge as a specific profession in the United States until the early years of the 20th century. Before that time, engineers, scientists, and researchers completed any necessary writing on their own.

During the early 1900s, technology expanded rapidly. The use of machines to manufacture and mass-produce a wide number of products paved the way for more complex and technical products. Scientists and researchers were discovering new technologies and applications for technology, particularly in electronics, medicine, and engineering. The need to record studies and research, and report them to others, grew. Also, as products became more complex, it was necessary to

QUICK FACTS

School Subjects
Business
English

Personal Skills
Communication/ideas
Technical/scientific

Work Environment
Primarily indoors
Primarily one location

Minimum Education Level
Bachelor's degree

Salary Range
$35,520 to $66,240 to $91,720+

Certification or Licensing
None available

Outlook
Faster than the average

DOT
131, 132

GOE
01.02.01

NOC
5121, 5122

O*NET-SOC
27-3041.00, 27-3042.00, 27-3043.00

provide information that documented their components, showed how they were assembled, and explained how to install, use, and repair them. By the mid-1920s, writers were being used to help engineers and scientists document their work and prepare technical information for nontechnical audiences.

Editors had been used for many years to work with printers and authors. They check copies of a printed document to correct any errors made during printing, to rewrite unclear passages, and to correct errors in spelling, grammar, and punctuation. As the need for technical writers grew, so too did the need for technical editors. Editors became more involved in documents before the printing stage, and today work closely with writers as they prepare their materials. Many editors coordinate the activities of all the people involved in preparing technical communications and manage the document development and production processes.

The need for technical writers grew further with the growth of the computer industry beginning in the 1960s. Originally, many computer companies used computer programmers to write user manuals and other documentation. It was widely assumed that the material was so complex that only those who were involved with creating computer programs would be able to write about them. Although computer programmers had the technical knowledge, many were not able to write clear, easy-to-use manuals. Complaints about the difficulty of using and understanding manuals were common. By the 1970s, computer companies began to hire technical writers to write computer manuals and documents. Today, this is one of the largest areas in which technical writers are employed.

The need for technical marketing writers also grew as a result of expanding computer technology. Many copywriters who worked for advertising agencies and marketing firms did not have the technical background to be able to describe the features of the technical products that were coming to market. Thus, a need for writers who could combine the ability to promote products with the ability to communicate technical information developed during this period.

The nature of technical writers' and technical editors' jobs continues to change with emerging technologies. Today, the ability to store, transmit, and receive information through computers and electronic means is changing the very nature of documents. Traditional books and paper documents are being replaced by Zip disks, CD-ROMs, wireless reading devices, interactive multimedia documents, and material accessed through bulletin board systems, faxes, the World Wide Web, and the Internet.

The telecommunications industry is just one of many rewarding employment options for technical writers and editors. Voice, video, and Internet communication systems have never been more complicated than they are today. Skilled writers are needed to translate complicated engineering, computer, and scientific concepts so that they can be understood by installers and repairers (who might need to consult technical specifications for a product in the field); non-technical workers in the industry, including customer service representatives, computer support specialists, and marketing and advertising specialists; and the general public, which needs comprehensible and accurate information about how to utilize these emerging and evolving communication devices and systems.

THE JOB

Technical writers and editors prepare a wide variety of documents and materials. The most common types of documents they produce are manuals, technical reports, specifications, and proposals. Some technical writers also write scripts for videos and audiovisual presentations and text for multimedia programs. Technical writers and editors prepare manuals that give instructions and detailed information on how to install, assemble, use, service, or repair a product or equipment (such as a cell phone, router, high-definition receiver, or firewall). They may write and edit manuals as simple as a two-page leaflet that gives instructions on how to turn on a cable box or as complex as a 500-page document that tells service technicians how to repair switching machinery, equipment at a call phone tower, or another system. One of the most common types of manuals is the computer software manual, which informs users on how to load software on their computers, explains how to use the program, and gives information on different features.

Technical writers and editors also prepare technical reports on a multitude of subjects. These reports include documents that give the results of research and laboratory tests and documents that describe the progress of a project. An example of this type of work might be a report on the effects of cell phone radiation on users over an extended period of time. They also write and edit sales proposals, product specifications, quality standards, journal articles, in-house style manuals, and newsletters.

The work of a technical writer begins when he or she is assigned to prepare a document. The writer meets with members of an account or technical team to learn the requirements for the document, the intended purpose or objectives, and the audience.

During the planning stage, the writer learns when the document needs to be completed, approximately how long it should be, whether artwork or illustrations are to be included, who the other team members are, and any other production or printing requirements. A schedule is created that defines the different stages of development and determines when the writer needs to have certain parts of the document ready.

The next step in document development is the research, or information gathering, phase. During this stage, technical writers gather all the available information about the product. For example, a technical writer might gather all the relevant information about a new personal digital assistant that is being developed by a cell phone company and, then, read and review this material and determine what other information should be obtained. They may research the topic by reading technical publications, but in most cases they will need to gather information directly from the people working on the product. Writers meet with and interview people who are sources of information, such as scientists, engineers, software developers, computer programmers, managers, and project managers. They ask questions, listen, and take notes or record interviews. They gather any available notes, drawings, or diagrams that may be useful.

After writers gather all the necessary information, they sort it out and organize it. They plan how they are going to present the information and prepare an outline for the document. They may decide how the document will look and prepare the design, format, and layout of the pages. In some cases, this may be done by an editor rather than the writer. If illustrations, diagrams, or photographs are going to be included, either the editor or writer makes arrangements for an illustrator, photographer, or art researcher to produce or obtain them.

Then, the writer starts writing and prepares a rough draft of the document. If the document is very large, a writer may prepare it in segments. Once the rough draft is completed, it is submitted to a designated person or group for technical review. Copies of the draft are distributed to managers, engineers, or other experts who can easily determine if any technical information is inaccurate or missing. These reviewers read the document and suggest changes.

The rough draft is also given to technical editors for review of a variety of elements. The editors check that the material is well-organized, that each section flows with the section before and after it, and that the language is appropriate for the intended audience (scientists, engineers, a company's CEO or board of directors, etc.). They also check for correct use of grammar, spelling, and punctuation. They ensure that names of parts or objects are consistent throughout the document and that references are accurate. They also check the labeling of graphs and captions for accuracy. Technical editors use special symbols, called proofreader's marks, to indicate the types of changes needed.

The editor and reviewers return their copies of the document to the technical writer. The writer incorporates the appropriate suggestions and revisions and prepares the final draft. The final draft is once again submitted to a designated reviewer or team of reviewers. In some cases, the technical reviewer may do a quick check to make sure that the requested changes were made. In other cases, the technical reviewer may examine the document in depth to ensure technical accuracy and correctness. A walkthrough, or test of the document, may be done for certain types of documents. For example, a walkthrough may be done for a document that explains how to install or activate a product. A tester installs or activates the product by following the instructions given in the document. The tester makes a note of all sections that are unclear or inaccurate, and the document is returned to the writer for any necessary revisions.

Once the final draft has been approved, the document is submitted to the technical editor, who makes a comprehensive check of the document. In addition to checking that the language is clear and reads smoothly, the editor ensures that the table of contents matches the different sections or chapters of a document, all illustrations and diagrams are correctly placed, all captions are matched to the correct picture, consistent terminology is used, and correct references are used in the bibliography and text.

The editor returns the document to either the *writer* or a *word processor*, who makes any necessary corrections. This copy is then checked by a *proofreader*. The proofreader compares the final copy against the editor's marked-up copy and makes sure that all changes were made. The document is then prepared for printing. In some cases, the writer is responsible for preparing camera-ready copy or electronic files for printing purposes, and in other cases, a print production coordinator prepares all material to submit to a printer.

Some technical writers specialize in a specific type of material. *Technical marketing writers* create promotional and marketing materials for technological products. They may write the copy for an advertisement for a technical product, such as a cell phone, high-definition satellite receiver, computer workstation or software, or they may write press releases about the product. They also write sales literature, product flyers, Web pages, and multimedia presentations.

Other technical writers prepare scripts for videos and films about technical subjects. These writers, called *scriptwriters*, need to have an understanding of film and video production techniques.

Some technical writers and editors prepare articles for scientific, computer, or engineering trade journals. These articles may report the results of research conducted by scientists or engineers or report on technological advances in a particular field. Some technical writers and editors also develop textbooks. They may receive articles written by engineers or scientists and edit and revise them to make them more suitable for the intended audience.

Technical writers and editors may create documents for a variety of media. Electronic media, such as compact discs and online services, are increasingly being used in place of books and paper documents. Technical writers may create materials that are accessed through bulletin board systems and the Internet or create computer-based resources, such as help menus on computer programs. They also create interactive, multimedia documents that are distributed on compact discs or floppy disks. Some of these media require knowledge of special computer programs that allow material to be hyperlinked, or electronically cross-referenced.

REQUIREMENTS

High School
In high school, you should take composition, grammar, literature, creative writing, journalism, social studies, math, statistics, engineering, computer science, and as many science classes as possible. Business courses are also useful as they explain the organizational structure of companies and how they operate.

Postsecondary Training
Most employers prefer to hire technical writers and editors who have a bachelor's or advanced degree. Many technical editors graduate with degrees in the humanities, especially English or journalism. Technical writers typically need to have a strong foundation in engineering, computers, or science, especially if they plan to work in a field such as telecommunications. Many technical writers graduate with a degree in engineering or science and take classes in technical writing. Some technical writers have degrees in telecommunications or a related field.

Many different types of college programs are available that prepare people to become technical writers and editors. A growing number of colleges are offering degrees in technical writing. Schools without a technical writing program may offer degrees in journalism or English. Programs are offered through English, communications, and journalism departments. Classes vary based on the type of program. In general, classes for technical writers include a core curriculum in writing and classes in algebra, statistics, logic, science, engineering, and computer programming languages. Useful classes for editors include technical writing, project management, grammar, proofreading, copyediting, and print production.

Many technical writers and editors earn a master's degree. In these programs, they study technical writing in depth and may specialize in a certain area, such as scriptwriting, instructional design, or multimedia applications. In addition, many nondegree writing programs are offered to technical writers and editors to hone their skills. Offered as extension courses or continuing education courses, these programs include courses on indexing, writing for trade journals, and other related subjects.

Technical writers, and occasionally technical editors, are often asked to present samples of their work. College students should build a portfolio during their college years in which they collect their best samples from work that they may have done for a literary magazine, newsletter, or yearbook.

Technical writers and editors should be willing to pursue learning throughout their careers. As technology changes, technical writers and editors may need to take classes to update their knowledge. Changes in electronic printing and computer technology will also change the way technical writers and editors do their jobs, and writers and editors may need to take courses to learn new skills or new technologies.

Other Requirements

Technical writers need to have good communications skills, science and technical aptitudes, and the ability to think analytically. Technical editors also need to have good communications skills, and judgment, as well as the ability to identify and correct errors in written material. They need to be diplomatic, assertive, and able to explain tactfully what needs to be corrected to writers, engineers, and other people involved with a document. Technical editors should be able to understand technical information easily, but they need less scientific and technical background than writers. Both technical writers and editors need to be able to work as part of a team and collaborate with others on a project. They need to be highly self-motivated, well organized, and able to work under pressure.

EXPLORING

If you enjoy writing and are considering a career in technical writing or editing, you should make writing a daily activity. Writing is a skill that develops over time and through practice. You can keep journals, join writing clubs, and practice different types of writing, such as scriptwriting and informative reports. Sharing writing with others and asking them to critique it is especially helpful. Comments from readers on what they enjoyed about a piece of writing or difficulty they had in understanding certain sections provides valuable feedback that helps to improve your writing style.

Reading a variety of materials is also helpful. Reading exposes you to both good and bad writing styles and techniques, and helps you to identify why one approach works better than another.

You may also gain experience by working on a literary magazine, student newspaper, or yearbook (or starting one of your own if one is not available). Both writing and editing articles and managing production give you the opportunity to learn new skills and to see what is involved in preparing documents and other materials.

Students may also be able to get internships, cooperative education assignments, or summer or part-time jobs as proofreaders or editorial assistants that may include writing responsibilities.

EMPLOYERS

There are approximately 49,000 technical writers currently employed in the United States; only a small percentage are employed in the telecommunications industry. Editors of all types (including technical editors) hold 122,000 jobs. Major telecommunications companies that employ technical writers and editors include Qualcomm, AT&T, Verizon, Motorola, Nokia, Sony, Comcast Cable Communications, Time Warner Cable, Cox Communications, DirecTV, and Dish Network Services.

Additionally, employment may be found in many different types of places, such as in the fields of aerospace, computers, engineering, pharmaceuticals, and research and development, or with the nuclear industry, medical publishers, government agencies or contractors, and colleges and universities. The aerospace, engineering, medical, and computer industries hire significant numbers of technical writers and editors. The federal government, particularly the Departments of Defense and Agriculture, the National Aeronautics and Space Administration (NASA), and the Atomic Energy Commission (AEC), also hires many writers and editors with technical knowledge.

STARTING OUT

Many technical writers start their careers as scientists, engineers, technicians, or research assistants and move into writing after several years of experience in those positions. Technical writers with a bachelor's degree in a technical subject such as engineering or computer science may be able to find work as a technical writer immediately upon graduating from college, but many employers prefer to hire writers with some work experience.

Technical editors who graduate with a bachelor's degree in English or journalism may find entry-level work as editorial assistants, copy editors, or proofreaders. From these positions, they are able to move into technical editing positions. Alternatively, beginning workers may find jobs as technical editors in small companies or those with a small technical communications department.

If you plan to work for the federal government, you need to pass an examination. Information about examinations and job openings is available at federal employment centers.

You may learn about job openings through your college's career services office and want ads in newspapers and professional magazines. You may also research companies that hire technical writers and editors and apply directly to them. Many libraries provide useful job resource guides and directories that provide information about companies that hire in specific areas.

ADVANCEMENT

As technical writers and editors gain experience, they move into more challenging and responsible positions. At first, they may work on simple documents or are assigned to work on sections of a document. As they demonstrate their proficiency and skills, they are given more complex assignments and are responsible for more activities.

Technical writers and editors with several years of experience may move into project management positions. As project managers, they are responsible for the entire document development and production processes. They schedule and budget resources and assign writers, editors, illustrators, and other workers to a project. They monitor the schedule, supervise workers, and ensure that costs remain in budget.

Technical writers and editors who show good project management skills, leadership abilities, and good interpersonal skills may become supervisors or managers. Both technical writers and editors can move into senior writer and senior editor positions. These positions involve increased responsibilities and may include supervising other workers.

Many technical writers and editors seek to develop and perfect their skills rather than move into management or supervisory positions. As they gain a reputation for their quality of work, they may be able to select choice assignments. They may learn new skills as a means of being able to work in new areas. For example, a technical writer may learn a new desktop program in order to become more proficient in designing. Or, a technical writer may learn a hypermedia or hypertext computer program in order to be able to create a multimedia program. Technical writers and editors who broaden their skill base and capabilities can move to higher-paying positions within their own company or at another company. They also may work as freelancers or set up their own communications companies.

EARNINGS

Mean annual earnings for salaried technical writers employed in the telecommunications industry were $66,240 in 2006, according to the U.S. Department of Labor. Salaries for all technical writers ranged from less than $35,520 to more than $91,720. Editors of all types earned a median salary of $46,990 in 2006. The lowest paid 10 percent earned $27,340 or less and the highest paid 10 percent earned $87,400 or more.

Most companies offer benefits that include paid holidays and vacations, medical insurance, and 401(k) plans. They may also offer profit sharing, pension plans, and tuition assistance programs.

WORK ENVIRONMENT

Technical writers and editors usually work in an office environment, with well-lit and quiet surroundings. They may have their own offices or share workspace with other writers and editors. Most writers and editors have computers. They may be able to utilize the services of support staff who can word process revisions, run off copies, fax material, and perform other administrative functions or they may have to perform all of these tasks themselves.

Some technical writers and editors work out of home offices and use computer modems and networks to send and receive materials electronically. They may go into the office only on occasion for meetings and gathering information. Freelancers and contract workers may work at a company's premises or at home.

Although the standard workweek is 40 hours, many technical writers and editors frequently work 50 or 60 hours a week. Job interruptions, meetings, and conferences can prevent writers from having long periods of time to write. Therefore, many writers work after hours or bring work home. Both writers and editors frequently work in the evening or on weekends in order to meet a deadline.

In many companies, there is pressure to produce documents as quickly as possible. Both technical writers and editors may feel at times that they are compromising the quality of their work due to the need to conform to time and budget constraints. In some companies, technical writers and editors may have increased workloads due to company reorganizations or downsizing. They may need to do the work that was formerly done by more than one person. Technical writers and editors also are increasingly assuming roles and responsibilities formerly performed by other people and this can increase work pressures and stress.

Despite these pressures, most technical writers and editors gain immense satisfaction from their work and the roles that they perform in producing technical communications.

OUTLOOK

The writing and editing field is generally very competitive, regardless of the industry. Each year, there are more people trying to enter this field than there are available openings. The field of technical writing and editing, though, offers more opportunities than other areas of writing and editing, such as book publishing or journalism. Employment opportunities for technical writers and editors are expected to grow faster than the average for all occupations through 2016, according to the U.S. Department of Labor,. Demand is growing for technical writers who can produce well-written computer manuals. Rapid growth in the high technology field, electronics industries, and the Internet will create a continuing demand for people to write users' guides, instruction manuals, and training materials. Technical writers will be needed to produce copy that describes developments and discoveries in law, science, and technology for a more general audience.

Technical writers will also be in demand in the telecommunications industry to write and edit materials for a wide range of audiences—from scientists and engineers; to technicians, installers, and repairers; to customers.

Writers may find positions that include duties in addition to writing. A growing trend is for companies to use writers to run a department, supervise other writers, and manage freelance writers and outside contractors. In addition, many writers are acquiring responsibilities that include desktop publishing and print production coordination.

The demand for technical writers and editors is significantly affected by the economy. During recessionary times, technical writers and editors are often among the first to be laid off. Many companies today are continuing to downsize or reduce their number of employees and are reluctant to keep writers on staff. Such companies prefer to hire writers and editors on a temporary contractual basis, using them only as long as it takes to complete an assigned document. Technical writers and editors who work on a temporary or freelance basis need to market their services and continually look for new assignments. They also do not have the security or benefits offered by full-time employment.

FOR MORE INFORMATION

For information on careers, contact
Society for Technical Communication
901 North Stuart Street, Suite 904
Arlington, VA 22203-1822
Tel: 703-522-4114
Email: stc@stc.org
http://www.stc.org

Telephone Operators

OVERVIEW

Telephone operators help people using phone company services, as well as other telephone operators, to place calls and to make connections. There are approximately 177,000 switchboard operators, 27,000 telephone operators, and 4,300 other communications equipment operators employed in the United States.

HISTORY

In the years since Alexander Graham Bell was granted a patent for his invention in 1876, the telephone has evolved from being a novelty gadget to an indispensable part of our daily lives. It is now possible to talk to someone in virtually any corner of the world on the telephone. Technological breakthroughs have allowed us to replace inefficient telephone cables with fiber optic lines and satellites for transmitting signals. Some phone features that we take for granted, such as conference calls, call waiting, and automatic call forwarding, have been developed only in the past few years.

Technology has also changed the job of the telephone operator. In the past, operators had to connect every phone call by hand, wrestling with hundreds of different cables and phone jacks and trying to match the person making the call to the number being dialed. Today, telephone switchboards are electronic, and the operator can connect many more calls by merely pushing buttons or dialing the proper code or number. Computers have replaced many of the old duties of telephone switchboard operators, such as

QUICK FACTS

School Subjects
Business
Speech

Personal Skills
Following instructions
Helping/teaching

Work Environment
Primarily indoors
Primarily one location

Minimum Education Level
High school diploma

Salary Range
$16,030 to $33,140 to
$46,670+

Certification or Licensing
None available

Outlook
Decline

DOT
235

GOE
09.06.01

NOC
1424

O*NET-SOC
43-2011.00, 43-2021.00,
43-2021.01, 43-2021.02

directory assistance and the "automatic intercept" of nonoperating numbers. Still, telephone operators are needed to perform special duties and add a human touch to telecommunications.

THE JOB

If you've recently made a collect call, checked your bank account balance over the phone, or left a message for someone in a large company, you may have done so without the assistance of an operator. With automation, computers, and voice synthesizers, you can now place a call directly and get all the information you need yourself, saving phone companies, and other businesses, time and money. The demand for telephone operators has dropped considerably from the days when operators were needed to physically connect and disconnect lines at a switchboard. AT&T has laid off thousands of operators in the last 20 years, but people can still find work with telecommunications companies and in corporations that handle a number of calls. Rynn Lemieux, an operator for the Hilton San Francisco, can remember the old "cord boards" from when she worked for an answering service more than 18 years ago. "I have to say," she says, "when you disconnected a call from one of those boards, you really knew you disconnected a call. Pushing a button just does not have the oomph of yanking a cord." Though Lemieux still works at a switchboard, she also uses a computer to find room numbers and in-house extensions. "I answer calls, connect to extensions and rooms, put in wake-up calls, as well as answer the TDD for the hearing impaired, page beepers, and answer questions concerning the city, the hotel, and pretty much anything else the caller can think of."

When a call comes into the phone company, a signal lights up on the switchboard, and the telephone operator makes the connection for it by pressing the proper buttons and dialing the proper numbers. If the person is calling from a pay phone, the operator may consult charts to determine the charges and ask the caller to deposit the correct amount to complete the call. If the customer requests a long-distance connection, the operator calculates and quotes the charges and then makes the connection.

Directory assistance operators, also called *information operators,* answer customer inquiries for local telephone numbers by using computerized alphabetical and geographical directories. The directory assistance operator types the spelling of the name requested and the possible location on a keyboard, then scans a directory to find the number. If the number can't be found, the operator may suggest alternate spellings of the name and look for phone numbers under those different spellings. When the name is located, the operator often doesn't need to read the number to the caller; instead, a computerized recording will provide the answer while the operator takes another call.

Telephone operators wear headsets that contain both an earphone and a microphone, leaving their hands free to operate the computer terminal or switchboard at which they are seated. They are supervised by *central-office-operator supervisors.*

Other types of switchboard supervisors perform advisory services for clients to show them how to get the most out of their phone systems. *Private branch exchange advisers* conduct training classes to demonstrate the operation of switchboard and teletype equipment, either at the telephone company's training school or on the customer's premises. They may analyze a company's telephone traffic loads and recommend the type of equipment and services that will best fit the company's needs. *Service observers* monitor the conversations between telephone operators and customers to observe the operators' behavior, technical skills, and adherence to phone company policies. Both of these types of workers may give advice on how operators can improve their handling of calls and their personal demeanor on the phone.

REQUIREMENTS

High School
You should take speech, drama, and other classes that will help you with oral communication skills. Typing and computer fundamentals courses will prepare you for the demands of running a modern switchboard and for handling special services such as TDD for the hearing impaired.

Postsecondary Training
Although a high school education is not a strict requirement for telephone operators, telephone companies prefer to hire people who are high school graduates. You're likely to receive most of your training from your employer, which may include classes in-house or telecommunications courses at a community college.

Certification or Licensing
Though a company may have its own training program leading to certification, there is no national certification. Many operators, however, do belong to local union chapters of such organizations as

Communications Workers of America (CWA). CWA assists workers in obtaining fair wages, benefits, and working conditions.

Other Requirements

Manual dexterity is an asset to the telephone operator; however, the degree of dexterity needed is about the same as that required for the operation of any type of office equipment. Personal qualifications should include tact, patience, a desire to work with people, and to be of service to others, a pleasing phone voice, an even-tempered disposition, and good judgment. Operators must also have legible handwriting and must be punctual and dependable in job attendance.

"A good memory for numbers helps," Rynn Lemieux says. "It's also good to know the city where you work."

EXPLORING

You can explore this career by arranging a visit to a local or long-distance telephone company to observe operators at work. There you may also have the chance to talk with operators about the job. You can also learn about new developments in telephone technology and services by visiting the Web site of the United States Telecom Association (http://www.usta.org).

Part-time office jobs may give students experience in working in-company phone exchanges and switchboards, in addition to general office experience. While telephone company operations are more complex, applicants with previous experience in handling phone calls may be given preference in hiring.

EMPLOYERS

Approximately 177,000 switchboard operators, 27,000 telephone operators, and 4,300 other communications equipment operators are employed in the United States. Operators are still needed in telephone companies, but most find jobs handling the phone lines of hotels, hospitals, retail stores, and other businesses with large numbers of employees. The customer service departments of companies and stores employ telephone operators to handle transactions, make courtesy calls, and answer customers' questions.

STARTING OUT

Individuals may enter this occupation by applying directly to telephone companies and long-distance carriers. In some cities, telephone offices maintain an employment office, while elsewhere employment interviews are conducted by a chief operator or personnel manager. Other job openings may be discovered through state or private employment agencies, newspaper advertisements, or school career services offices.

New telephone company employees are usually given a combination of classroom work and on-the-job practice. In the various telephone companies, classroom instruction usually lasts up to three weeks. The nation's time zones and geography are covered so that operators can understand how to calculate rates and know where major cities are located. Recordings are used to familiarize trainees with the various signals and tones of the phone system as well as give them the chance to hear their own phone voices and improve their diction and courtesy. Close supervision continues after training is completed.

Telephone operators continue to receive on-the-job training throughout their careers as phone offices install more modern and automated equipment and as the methods of working with the equipment continue to change. Service assistants are responsible for instructing the new operators in various other types of special operating services.

ADVANCEMENT

Telephone operators may have opportunities for advancement to positions as service assistant, and later to group or assistant chief operator. *Chief operators* are responsible for planning and directing the activities of a central office, as well as personnel functions and the performance of the employees. Service assistants may sometimes advance to become *PBX service advisors,* who go to individual businesses, assess their phone needs, and oversee equipment installation and employee training. Some telephone operators take other positions within a telephone company, such as a clerical position, and advance within that position.

Opportunities for advancement usually depend on the employee's personal initiative, ability, experience, length of employment, and job performance, as well as the size of the place of employment and the number of supervisors needed. Most telephone company operators are members of a union, and the union specifies the time and steps to advance from one position to another. However, many operators can become qualified for a higher-level position but then need to wait for years for an available opening. Some telephone operators become private branch exchange or switchboard operators in corporations and large businesses.

Lemieux advises that you consider a job as a telephone operator as a stepping stone. "If the telecommunications industry is what interests you," she says, "aim towards installation and/or repair with a large company. That's where the real money is, and where you'll find the most respect."

EARNINGS

The wages paid to telephone operators vary from state to state, from one section of the country to another, and even from city to city. The types of duties performed by the employee also affect the salary he or she earns.

According to the U.S. Department of Labor, median hourly earnings of switchboard operators, including answering service, were $10.88 in 2006. Wages ranged from less than $7.71 to more than $15.93 ($16,030 to $33,140 annually). Median hourly earnings of telephone operators in 2006 were $16.41, with wages ranging from less than $8.44 to more than $22.44 ($17,540 to $46,670 annually).

Operators are usually paid time-and-a-half for Sunday work and may receive an extra day's pay for working on legal holidays. Some additional remuneration is usually paid when employees work split shifts or shifts that end after 6:00 P.M. Time-and-a-half pay is generally given if operators work more than a five-day week. Choice of work hours is usually determined on the basis of seniority. Pay increases in most instances are determined on the basis of periodic pay scales.

Fringe benefits for these employees usually include paid annual vacations and group insurance plans for sickness, accident, and death; the majority also have retirement and disability pension plans available.

WORK ENVIRONMENT

The telephone industry operates around the clock giving the public 24-hour daily service. Operators may, therefore, be required to work evening hours, night shifts, and on Sundays and holidays. Some operators are asked to work split shifts to cover periods of heavy calling. Telephone company operators generally work 32.5 to 37.5 hours per week.

The telephone operator's job demands good physical health for punctual and regular job attendance; the work, however, is not physically strenuous or demanding. While working, operators are at the switchboard and are allowed to take periodic rest breaks. General working conditions are usually in pleasant surroundings with relatively little noise or confusion. Many telephone company operators work at computer or video monitors, which may cause eyestrain and muscle strain if not properly designed.

The work of a telephone operator can be very repetitive and is closely supervised. Calls are monitored by supervisors to check that operators are courteous and following company policies. Some operators find this stressful. In addition, telephone companies track the number of calls handled by each operator, and there is an increasing emphasis on operators handling a greater number of calls in order to improve cost efficiencies. This need for higher productivity can also create stress for some workers. Many times the atmosphere becomes stressful and hectic during peak calling times, and operators need to manage a high volume of calls without becoming distressed.

OUTLOOK

Employment of telephone operators is expected to decline through 2016, according to the U.S. Department of Labor. During the past 30 years, employment of operators in telephone companies has declined sharply due to automation, which increases the productivity of these workers. Direct dialing and computerized billing have eliminated the need for many operators. Voice recognition technology, which gives computers the capacity to understand speech and to respond to callers, now offers directory assistance and helps to place collect calls. Voice response equipment, which allows callers to communicate with computers through the use of touch-tone signals, is used widely by a number of large companies. Using a combination of voice response equipment, voice mail and messaging systems, and automated call distribution, incoming phone calls can be routed to their destination without the use of an operator. People now use the Internet and email to communicate, neither of which require operators. Directory assistance services are also available on the Internet and provide phone numbers, addresses, maps, and email addresses.

Operators will find most job opportunities outside the phone companies, with customer service departments, telemarketing firms, reservation ticket agencies, hotel switchboards, and other services that field a number of calls. TDD, phone services for the deaf, also requires operators, and the Americans with Disabilities Act (ADA) is allowing people with auditory, speech, and visual, and other physical disabilities better access to such services. Unions have tried to make sure that companies avoid job layoffs either through attrition or through retraining and reassigning workers. Many telephone companies, however, continue to make workforce reductions by eliminating telephone operator positions or by sending jobs to foreign countries in an attempt to cut operating costs to maintain and increase their profit margins in a competitive global telecommunications marketplace. There will be limited opportunities for employment as a telephone operator in the future.

FOR MORE INFORMATION

To learn about issues affecting jobs in telecommunications, visit the CWA's Web site.

Communications Workers of America (CWA)
501 Third Street, NW
Washington, DC 20001-2797
Tel: 202-434-1100
http://www.cwa-union.org

For information about telecommunication careers and new developments in telephone technology and services, contact

United States Telecom Association
607 14th Street NW Suite 400
Washington, DC 20005-2164
Tel: 202-326-7300
http://www.usta.org

Telephone and PBX Installers and Repairers

OVERVIEW

Telephone and private branch exchange (PBX) installers and repairers install, service, and repair telephone and PBX systems in customers' homes and places of business.

HISTORY

In 1876, the first practical device for transmitting speech over electric wires was patented by Alexander Graham Bell. The telephone device Bell invented functioned on essentially the same principle as the telephones that are familiar to us today. Both transmit the vibrations of speech sounds by transferring them to solid bodies and converting them to electrical impulses, which can travel along wires. However, technological advances in telephone systems over the past century have turned telephones into powerful instruments for communication.

Within a few years after its introduction, many customers were having the new devices installed and were being connected into local telephone systems. Four years after Bell's patent, there were 30,000 subscribers to 138 local telephone exchanges. By 1887, there were 150,000 telephones in the United States. Long distance service developed slowly because of problems with distortion and signal loss over longer transmission lines. Over time, advances such as amplifiers on transmission lines, microwave radio links, shortwave relays, undersea cables, and earth satellites that amplify and relay signals have so improved service that today's telephone customers expect that their telephone can be quickly linked to one of many millions of other telephones around the globe.

As telephones became a crucial part of 20th-century life, a need arose for workers who specialized in installing, removing, and repairing telephone instruments and related devices. However, today's technology has advanced to the point where fewer of these workers are needed than in the past. Once basic wiring is in place, customers can handle much of their own installation work, and telephones can be manufactured so cheaply that it is often simpler to replace instead of repair malfunctioning equipment.

THE JOB

When calls go from one telephone to another, they usually go through a telephone company facility that houses automatic switching equipment. For telephone calls to go through, an array of wires, cable, switches, transformers, and other equipment must be installed and in good operating order. *Central office workers, cable splicers, and line repairers* are among the workers who work on telephone equipment away from the customer's premises. *Telephone and PBX installers and repairers* are workers who service the systems on the customer's premises.

When customers request a new telephone line or equipment, *telephone installers,* also called *station installers,* do the necessary work. They often travel to the customer's home or business in a vehicle that contains a variety of tools and equipment. If they must make a new connection, they may have to work on roofs, ladders, or at the top of a telephone pole to attach an incoming wire to the service line. They install a terminal box and connect the appropriate wires. On some jobs, they may have to drill through walls or floors to run wiring. In large buildings, they may connect service wires or terminals in basements or wire closets. After installing equipment, they test it to make sure it functions as it should. Telephone installers may also install or remove telephone booths, coin collectors, and switching key equipment, in addition to private and business phones.

Wear and deterioration may cause telephones to function improperly. *Telephone repairers* can determine the cause of such problems, sometimes with the assistance of *testboard workers* or *trouble locators* in the central office, and then repair the problem and restore service.

Steve Markowsky installs and repairs residential telephones in upstate central New York for Alltel, a telecommunications company. When a customer has a problem, Markowsky receives the service order via computer. He then attempts to contact the customer by phone. If unable to reach the customer, he then goes to the customer's telephone interface—a box outside of the home. "With a telephone butt-in set," Markowsky says, "I can clip into the line and listen for a dial tone, and even place a call." If the problem is not with the outside line, Markowsky can assist customers on a per hour basis to find the problem within the home. "The trouble might be as simple as a phone off the hook." To locate the problem, Markowsky uses a bell meter to test the phone and outlet. "If the trouble isn't in the phone or the outlet, it's in the wire." Markowsky must replace wire on a daily basis.

"I carry a small number of hand tools," Markowsky says, "like screwdrivers, needle-nose pliers, side-cutters, rechargeable drill, a stapler made for stapling wires."

Some larger users of telephone services, such as some businesses or hotels, have a single telephone number. Calls that come in may be routed to the proper telephone with PBX switching equipment located on the customer's premises. Outgoing calls also go through what is in effect a private telephone system within the building. In addition to handling regular phone calls, PBX equipment is often used for specialized services such as electronic mail. *PBX installers*, also called *systems technicians*, set up the necessary wiring, switches, and other equipment to make the system function, often creating customized switchboards. These workers often work as part of a crew because the communications equipment they work with is heavy, bulky, and complex.

PBX repairers, with the assistance of *testboard workers*, locate malfunctions and repair PBX and other telephone systems. They may also maintain related equipment, such as power plants, batteries, and relays. Some PBX repairers service and repair mobile radiophones, microwave transmission equipment, and other sophisticated telecommunications devices and equipment.

Some experienced workers can handle a range of installation and repair work. They may put their skills to use handling special jobs, such as investigating unauthorized use of telephone equipment.

REQUIREMENTS

High School
Math courses will help you prepare for the technical nature of this career, along with voc-tech, electronics, and other courses that will involve you with hands-on experiments. Computer courses will also

be valuable. You should take English, speech, and other courses that will help you develop your communication skills.

Postsecondary Training
Telephone companies usually prefer to hire applicants who have no previous experience with another telephone company and then train the beginners to work with the equipment used in their own system. Companies generally prefer applicants who are high school or vocational school graduates and who have mechanical ability and manual dexterity. Some employers may require an associate's or bachelor's degree in an area such as engineering. Because of the rapid advancements of telecommunications technology, installers may be required to take continuing education courses, either as part of in-house training or through a college program.

Certification and Licensing
The Society of Cable Telecommunications Engineers and the Telecommunications Industry Association offer certification programs for telecommunications professionals. Contact the organizations for more information.

Other Requirements
Because installers and repairers deal with company customers, they should have a neat appearance and a pleasant manner. "I love to meet people," Markowsky says. "And I love problem solving. It's very gratifying work." Good eyesight and color vision are needed for working with small parts and for distinguishing the color-coding of wires. Good hearing is necessary for detecting malfunctions revealed by sound.

Many telephone employees are members of unions, and union membership may be required. The Communications Workers of America (CWA) and International Brotherhood of Electrical Workers (IBEW) are two unions which represent many workers.

EXPLORING
High school courses in physics, mathematics, blueprint reading, and shop can help you gauge your aptitudes and interest in these occupations. Try building electronic kits and assembling models to test your manual dexterity and mechanical ability and to provide you with experience in following drawings and plans. Direct work experience in this field is probably unavailable on a part-time or summer job basis, but it may be possible to arrange a visit to a telephone company facility to get an overall view of the company's operations.

A technician installs a telecommunication device for the deaf on a pay phone. *(Jeff Greenberg, The Image Works)*

EMPLOYERS

Telephone installers work for telecommunications companies. They also work for companies that provide phone equipment and services for hotels. Companies that install and service security systems for homes and businesses also employ installers.

STARTING OUT

Job seekers in this field should contact the employment offices of local telephone companies. Pre-employment tests may be given to determine your knowledge and aptitude for the work.

Newly hired workers learn their skills in programs that last several months. The programs may combine on-the-job work experience with formal classroom instruction and self-instruction using materials such as videotapes, DVDs, and training manuals. Trainees practice such tasks as connecting telephones to service wires in classrooms that simulate real working conditions. They also accompany experienced workers to job sites and observe them as they work. After they have learned how to install telephone equipment, workers need additional training to become telephone repairers, PBX installers, or PBX repairers.

If there are no openings in the training program at the time they are hired, new workers are assigned instead to some other type of job until openings develop. It is common for openings for installer and repairer positions to be filled by workers who are already employed in other jobs with the same company. In the future, it probably will be even more difficult for workers coming in from outside to get these jobs.

ADVANCEMENT

More experienced telephone installers may, with additional training, move into jobs as PBX installers or as telephone repairers. Similarly, additional training may allow telephone repairers to become PBX repairers. Some experienced workers become *installer-repairers*, combining installation and repair work on telephone company or PBX systems. Some workers may advance to supervisory positions, in which they coordinate and direct the activities of other installers or repairers.

EARNINGS

In comparison with workers in other craft fields, telephone and PBX installers and repairers are generally well paid. Their actual pay rates vary with their job responsibilities, geographical region, their length of service with the company, and other factors. According to the U.S. Department of Labor, mean annual earnings of telecommunications equipment installers and repairers employed by wired telecommunications carriers were $53,840 in 2006. Earnings for all telecommunications equipment installers and repairers ranged from less than $31,110 to $68,310 or more. Workers in this occupation generally have a low turnover rate, therefore, many workers are in the higher wage categories. Fringe benefits for these workers usually include paid holidays and vacations, sick leave, health and disability insurance, and retirement plans.

WORK ENVIRONMENT

Telephone installers and repairers often do their work independently, with a minimum of supervision. Especially during emergency situations they may need to work at night, on weekends, or on holidays to restore service. Most installers are on-call 24 hours a day. Most of the work is done in the field in the homes and offices of clients.

Some installation work is done outside, including work on poles, ladders, and rooftops, and some work requires stooping, bending, reaching, and working in awkward or cramped positions. "I work outside in the elements every day," Markowsky says. "I'm exposed to all sorts of weather. Last year, I was involved with the unbelievable devastation of an ice storm in upstate New York. Thousands of phone lines came down. Those were long hours and long weeks."

PBX installers and repairers frequently work as part of crews. Most of their work is indoors, and it may involve crouching, crawling, and lifting.

OUTLOOK

Employment of telecommunications equipment installers and repairers is expected to experience little or no change through 2016, according to the U.S. Department of Labor. Jobs will be available as telecommunications companies upgrade internal lines in businesses and homes and wire new homes with fiber optic lines. The wide use of the Internet and fax machines has led to a number of homes with multiple lines. Because much business is now conducted through telephone lines, repairs during storms and other emergencies must be done more quickly and efficiently, requiring the skills of experienced installers and repairers.

Central office and PBX installers and repairers experienced in current technology should find employment opportunities, due to a growing demand for telecommunications networks that offer multimedia services such as VoIP (Voice over Internet Protocol) and video on demand.

Factors that will limit employment growth include sweeping technological changes that are making it possible to install and maintain phone systems with far fewer workers than in the past. In addition, new computerized systems are very reliable and have self-diagnosing features that make it easy for repairers to locate problems and replace defective parts. As older, less reliable equipment is taken out of service and new equipment is installed in its place, the need for repairers and installers will decline even further.

Installers and repairers with additional training may be able to find work with the growing number of businesses that connect office computers and networks. Those with degrees in engineering can assist in the design for the cabling of business complexes, colleges, and other institutions requiring up-to-date communication services.

FOR MORE INFORMATION

For information about unions and job opportunities, contact
Communications Workers of America
501 Third Street, NW
Washington, DC 20001-2797
Tel: 202-434-1100
http://www.cwa-union.org

For information on union membership, contact
International Brotherhood of Electrical Workers
900 Seventh Street, NW
Washington DC 20001-3886
Tel: 202-833-7000
http://ibew.org

For information on careers, educational programs, educational seminars, distance learning, and certification, contact
Society of Cable Telecommunications Engineers
140 Philips Road
Exton, PA 19341-1318
Tel: 800-542-5040
Email: scte@scte.org
http://www.scte.org

For information about conferences, special programs, and member-ship, contact

Women in Cable and Telecommunications
14555 Avion Parkway, Suite 250
Chantilly, VA 20151-1117
Tel: 703-234-9810
http://www.wict.org

Wireless Sales Workers

OVERVIEW

Wireless sales workers, also known as *wireless* or *cellular sales representatives,* work for wireless telecommunications service providers to sell products and services to individuals and businesses. The products and services they sell include cellular phones, phone service, pagers, paging service, and various wireless service package options. Inside sales workers work on-site at their employers' sales offices, helping customers who come in to inquire about wireless service. Outside sales workers travel to call on various potential customers at their offices.

HISTORY

Although you may think of cellular phones as being a product of late 20th century technology, they actually have their beginnings all the way back in the late 1800s. In 1895, an Italian electrical engineer and inventor named Guglielmo Marconi figured out how to transmit signals from one place to another using electromagnetic waves, creating the first radio. One of Marconi's first major successes came in 1896, when he was able to send signals over a distance of more than a mile. Marconi continued to improve and refine his invention. In 1897, he transmitted signals from shore to a ship at sea 18 miles away, and in 1901, he sent signals a distance of 200 miles. By 1905, many ships were regularly using Marconi's radio to communicate with the shore.

Radio evolved rapidly. By the mid-1920s, more than 1,400 radio stations were broadcasting programming all across America, and by the end of the 1940s, that number had grown to 2,020. Immediately following World War II, radio saw a period of especially rapid development and improvement. Sophisticated transmitting and receiving equipment played a key role in the exploration of space, and in 1969, astronauts on the Apollo mission used a very high-frequency radio communication system to transmit their voices from the Moon back to Earth for the first time.

Cellular radio, which is essentially today's cellular phone service, was first tested in the United States in the 1970s. This system, a miniature version of large radio networks, was named cellular because its broadcast area is divided into units called cells. Each cell was equipped with its own radio transmitter, with a range of about 1 to 2.5 miles. As a mobile radiophone moved through this network of cells, its calls were switched from one cell to another by a computerized system. It was possible to make calls only within the area covered by the network of cells, however; once the radiophone was outside the cellular area, the connection was lost. First tested in Chicago and the Washington, D.C., area, this cellular system was soon duplicated in other towns, both large and small, throughout the United States. As more and more of the United States became covered with these networks of cells, it became possible to use cellular phones in more places and use of these phones became increasingly widespread.

In order to use a cellular phone, one had to have two things: the phone itself and a subscription to a cellular service. Cellular service providers, much like traditional phone companies, signed users up for phone service to be billed on a monthly basis. Often, as part of the sign-up agreement, the new customer received a free or inexpensive cellular phone. As the availability of cellular service has expanded geographically, the number of people signing up for this service has increased dramatically. According to CTIA-The Wireless Association, in 2007 more than 243 million Americans were wireless service subscribers. Cellular, or wireless, sales workers in communities across the United States have been the liaison between the cellular providers and the cellular users. They have been the workers selling the service, explaining its workings, and signing up these new users.

THE JOB

Wireless sales workers sell communications systems, equipment, and services to both businesses and individuals. The products they sell may be divided up into "hard" products—such as pagers or cellular phones—and "soft" products, such as cellular phone service, paging service, voice mail, or phone service options. Most wireless sales workers work for a cellular service provider, trying to persuade prospective buyers to sign up for that provider's phone service. In areas that are covered by two or more cellular providers, the salesperson may have to convince customers to use his or her provider instead of the competition. In other cases, it is merely a matter of convincing the customer that he or she needs cellular service, explaining what the service provides, and doing the paperwork to begin a contract.

There are two categories of wireless sales workers. Outside sales workers visit prospective clients at their offices. These workers may make appointments in advance, or they may drop in unannounced and ask for a few minutes of the prospective customer's time. This practice is called cold calling. Outside sales workers often call on customers only within a specific geographic territory that may be defined by their employers. Members of the second category, inside sales workers, work in a cellular provider's offices, frequently in a customer showroom. These workers greet and help customers who come into the office to buy or inquire about wireless services. Brian Quigley is the inside sales manager for a major cellular service provider in Bloomington, Indiana. Before becoming the manager, he worked as a sales representative for four years.

There are several aspects of a wireless sales representative's job. The first is generating new customers. Sales workers develop lists of possible customers in many different ways. They may ask for referrals from existing customers, call on new businesses or individuals as they move into their assigned territory, or compile names and numbers from business directories or phone books. They may also attend business trade shows or expositions, or join networking groups where they can make contact with people who might be interested in signing up for their service. Once sales workers have their list of possible contacts, they may send out letters or sales brochures, often following up with a phone call and a request for an appointment.

The second aspect of the job is perhaps the most important. This involves talking with prospective customers about the company's services and products and helping them choose the ones that they will be happy with. In order to do this, the sales worker must have a thorough knowledge of all the company's offerings and be

A sales worker explains a cell phone's features to a customer. (*John Bazemore, Associated Press*)

able to explain how these offerings can meet the customer's needs. "We spend a lot of time each day taking sales calls from people or working with walk-ins," Quigley says. "And dealing with people who are considering buying wireless is not a quick process. On the average, you spend between 15 and 30 minutes with one customer, answering all of his or her questions." Answering these questions may involve demonstrating the features of different phones or pagers, going over the pricing structures of various service plans, or explaining how the wireless service works and what its geographic limitations are. The sales worker must try to overcome any objections the customer might have about the products or services and convince him or her to make the purchase. If the salesperson fails to "close the deal" on the first visit, he or she might follow up with more visits, phone calls, or letters.

A wireless sales worker's job usually involves a certain amount of paperwork. When a salesperson makes a sale, he or she may input the customer's billing and credit information into a computer in order to generate a contract, explain the contract to the customer, and ask him or her to sign it. He or she may also do the paperwork necessary to activate the new customer's phone or pager. Sales workers may also maintain records on all their customers, usually in a computer database.

Many sales workers maintain contact with their customers even after making a sale. The salesperson may make a follow-up call to ensure that the customer's service or product is working properly and that he or she is satisfied. The salesperson may also check back periodically to see if the customer is interested in purchasing "upgrades"—new or improved services or products. The sales reps in Quigley's location also help existing customers who have questions about their equipment, service, or billing statement. "You'd be surprised how much of my job is servicing existing customers," he says. "I'll bet I spend 80 percent of my time on customer retention."

Because wireless technology changes so rapidly, learning about new products and services is an important part of a wireless sales worker's job. He or she may frequently attend seminars or training programs to keep current on the latest in wireless products, in order to be able to explain them to potential customers. Quigley says that his company holds quarterly sales rallies, where wireless equipment manufacturers come to explain and demonstrate their new products. "A lot of the stuff you just have to learn on your own, too," he says. "Because things change so rapidly, you often can't wait until the next sales rally to find out about a piece of equipment. You just have to crack open the manual and read up on it."

REQUIREMENTS

High School
The minimum educational level needed to become a wireless sales worker is a high school diploma. To prepare for a career in wireless sales, you should choose high school classes that will help you understand and communicate with people. Courses in speech, English, and psychology are all good options for this. You might also want to take classes that help you understand basic business principles, such as business and math courses. Finally, it may be helpful to take some fundamental computer classes in order to become familiar with keyboarding and using some basic software applications. Like virtually all other offices, wireless offices are typically computerized so you will probably need to be comfortable using a computer.

Postsecondary Training

Although there are no formal requirements, it is becoming more and more common for wireless sales workers to have a two- or four-year college degree. Brian Quigley began his career in wireless sales after obtaining a bachelor's degree in marketing, and he says that his company prefers to recruit college graduates. Many employers consider a bachelor's degree in marketing, business, or telecommunications to be especially beneficial. In addition, because wireless services are so heavily dependent on technology, some wireless sales workers enter the field with a technology-related degree.

Whether a new wireless sales worker has a college degree or not, there are likely to be aspects of the job and the company that he or she is not familiar with. Therefore, most wireless service companies provide training programs for their newly hired workers. These programs, which may last from three weeks to three months, cover such topics as cellular technologies, product lines, sales techniques, using the company's computer system, entering orders, and other company policies.

Other Requirements

Successful wireless sales workers have a combination of personal characteristics that allow them to do their jobs well. Perhaps the most important is the ability to connect and communicate with people; without this quality, it is virtually impossible to be an effective salesperson. Wireless salespersons should enjoy interacting with people, feel comfortable talking with people they do not know, and be able to communicate clearly and persuasively. "You also have to be a good listener, in addition to a good talker," Quigley says. "When someone is upset, you have to hear what they are saying and be able to appease them." The ability to work in a high-pressure, competitive environment is also an important characteristic. Many wireless sales workers earn the majority of their income from commissions or bonuses. In addition, most workers are expected to meet monthly or quarterly sales goals that are set by the company. Successful sales workers should be able to handle the stress of working to meet these goals. Self-confidence is another essential quality of good sales workers. Any sales job will involve a certain amount of rejection from customers who are not interested or not ready to buy. Salespersons must be secure and confident enough to avoid letting this rejection affect them on a personal level. According to Quigley, the willingness to learn and change is also highly important to success in this field.

"This industry is always changing, sometimes so quickly that it's hard to keep up with it," he says. "You have to be prepared for the changes."

EXPLORING

You can find out what it is like to be a wireless sales worker by visiting the offices of a local cellular provider. By talking with the sales staff and perhaps observing them as they work, you should be able to get a feel for what the day-to-day job entails. One of the best ways to find out firsthand if you enjoy selling is to find a summer or after-school job in sales. To learn more about wireless technology and the products available, visit your local library and see what books and magazine articles are available—or do some online research, if you have access to the Internet.

EMPLOYERS

Most of the major telecommunications companies throughout the United States offer wireless service in addition to their traditional phone service. For example, AT&T, Sprint Nextel, MCI, Verizon, and U.S. Cellular all have wireless divisions—and, consequently, wireless sales staff. These providers are located all throughout the United States, in virtually every medium-sized and large community. You should be able to find a list of them by asking your local librarian for help or by doing a keyword search on "wireless service providers" on the Internet.

STARTING OUT

To find a job in wireless sales, you should first determine which wireless service providers operate in your area. Check directly with these providers to find out if they have any openings, or send them a resume and cover letter. If you are willing to relocate, you might contact the national headquarters of each of the large wireless companies mentioned earlier to find out what jobs are available nationwide. Many of these companies even have Web sites that list current job openings. You might also keep an eye on local or regional newspapers. Telecommunications companies, including wireless providers, frequently post job openings in the classified sections of these newspapers. If you have attended a college or university, check with your school's career services office to see if it has any contacts with wireless service providers.

Many wireless providers prefer to hire applicants with proven sales records. This may be especially true in cases where the applicant has only a high school diploma. If you find that you are having difficulty obtaining a position in wireless sales, you might consider first taking another sales job (perhaps in electronic or communications equipment) to gain experience. Once you have proven your abilities, you may have better luck being hired for a wireless sales position.

ADVANCEMENT

For most wireless salespersons, advancement comes in the form of increased income via commissions and bonuses. A proven sales worker might earn the title of *senior sales representative* or *senior account executive.* These workers may be given better territories or larger, more important accounts to handle. Some sales workers eventually move into managerial roles as they expand in their capabilities and knowledge of the company. A sales worker might move into the position of *sales manager,* for example. In this position, he or she would oversee other salespersons, either for the entire organization or for a specific geographic territory. Quigley became the sales manager for his location after four years of working as a sales representative. The next step on the career ladder for him is *general*

Wireless Facts, 2007

- There were 243.3 million wireless subscribers in the United States.
- Nearly 13 percent of U.S. households were wireless only—meaning they did not have a land line.
- The wireless industry employed 257,000 people.
- Wireless industry revenues topped more than $134 billion.
- There were 210,360 cell sites—an increase of more than 90 percent since 1995.

Sources: CTIA-The Wireless Association, National Center for Health Statistics

manager of retail stores, which would put him in charge of a specific geographic region. Another advancement possibility in larger companies is that of *trainer.* In the role of sales trainer, a sales worker would be responsible for developing, coordinating, and training new employees in sales techniques.

EARNINGS

For motivated and skilled salespersons, the pay for wireless sales can be quite good. Most companies offer their sales staff a small base salary and incentive pay in the form of commissions, bonuses, or both. In some cases, the incentive pay can increase the salesperson's base salary by up to 75 percent. Because most salespersons earn the majority of their income through incentive pay, the income level depends greatly upon individual performance.

According to the *U.S. News & World Report*'s "Best Jobs for the Future," the average beginning wireless sales worker might expect to earn around $35,000 annually. A senior sales worker might earn around $68,000, and a top sales executive can make as much as $110,000. Wireless sales managers can expect to earn between $75,000 and $80,000 per year.

Sales workers who are employed by most wireless companies receive a benefits package, which typically includes health insurance and paid vacation, sick days, and holidays. Outside sales workers may be provided with a company car and an expense account to pay for food, lodging, and travel expenses incurred while traveling on company business.

WORK ENVIRONMENT

Inside sales representatives typically work in comfortable, attractively decorated customer showrooms. They usually have desks either in the showroom or in a back office, where they can do their paperwork and perhaps meet with customers. While many sales reps work regular 40-hour weeks, Monday through Friday, it is not at all uncommon for these workers to work longer-than-average weeks. In addition, many wireless sales offices are open on weekends to accommodate customers who cannot come in during the week. Therefore, some sales workers spend weekend hours at the office.

Outside sales workers may spend much of their time traveling to meet on-site with various potential customers. Unless a salesperson's territory is very large, however, overnight travel is uncommon.

When not traveling, outside sales workers may spend time in the office, setting up appointments with customers, keeping records, and completing paperwork. Both types of sales workers spend the majority of their time dealing with people. In addition to customer contact, these salespersons often work cooperatively with service technicians and customer service staff.

OUTLOOK

Job opportunities for wireless sales workers are expected to grow at a rate that is faster than the average. CTIA-The Wireless Association estimates that there are approximately 63,000 new wireless subscribers every day. The sales of pagers and paging services has also grown tremendously. Part of the reason for this growth is that technological advances are making wireless phones and pagers more effective and useful all the time. One of the most recent developments, digital communication technology, has increased wireless phone use by offering better quality and range (98 percent of all wireless subscribers are now digital). Wireless service is also being increasingly used to transmit data as well as voice. Examples of wireless data communication include such applications as texting, emailing, faxing, and Internet access. In addition, new technology, widespread use of wireless services, and more leverage for the consumer as a result of federal legislation (such as being able to change providers and keeping the same wireless phone number) have driven the prices of service down. This means that wireless services are now an option for many people who previously couldn't afford them. All of these factors combined should spur the need for a growing number of sales workers. The demand for jobs will also be enhanced by the high turnover in the sales field as a whole. Each year, many sales workers leave their jobs—in wireless and other industries—because they fail to make enough money or feel they are not well suited to this demanding career. New sales workers must then be hired to replace those who have left the field.

FOR MORE INFORMATION

For job postings, links to wireless industry recruiters, industry news, and training information, contact or visit the following Web site

CTIA-The Wireless Association
1400 16th Street, NW, Suite 600
Washington, DC 20036-2225

Tel: 202-785-0081
http://www.ctia.org

For the latest on the wireless industry and job information, contact
Wireless Industry Association
8290 West Sahara Avenue, Suite 260
Las Vegas, NV 89117-8931
Tel: 800-624-6918
Email: contact@wirelessindustry.com
https://wirelessindustry.com

For a brochure on mobile phone etiquette and other information on the wireless industry in Canada, contact or visit the following Web site
Canadian Wireless Telecommunications Association
130 Albert Street, Suite 1110
Ottawa, ON K1P 5G4 Canada
Tel: 613-233-4888
Email: info@cwta.ca
http://www.cwta.ca

Wireless Service Technicians

OVERVIEW

Wireless service technicians maintain a specified group of cell sites, including the radio towers, cell site equipment, and often the building and grounds for the sites. Technicians routinely visit and monitor the functioning of the on-site equipment, performing preventive testing and maintenance. They also troubleshoot and remedy problems that might arise with any of their sites. Most wireless service technicians spend their work time at various locations, visiting each of their cell sites as necessary.

HISTORY

The concept of cellular communication, as it is used today, was developed by Bell Laboratories in the late 1940s. However, it was based on a much older concept: using radio waves to transmit signals over distances. The concept of communicating via radio waves dates back to the late 1800s, when an Italian inventor named Guglielmo Marconi discovered that radio signals could be transmitted for more than a mile. By 1905, many ships at sea were routinely using Marconi's invention to communicate with the shore.

Cellular radio, which is essentially today's cellular phone service, was first tested in two U.S. markets in the 1970s. This system, a miniature version of large radio networks, was named "cellular" because its broadcast area is divided into smaller units called cells. Each cell was equipped with its own radio tower, with a range of between 1 and 2.5 miles. As a mobile "radiophone" moved through the network of

QUICK FACTS

School Subjects
Computer science
Physics

Personal Skills
Mechanical/manipulative
Technical/scientific

Work Environment
Primarily indoors
Primarily multiple locations

Minimum Education Level
Associate's degree

Salary Range
$31,110 to $49,050 to $68,310+

Certification or Licensing
None available

Outlook
More slowly than the average

DOT
722

GOE
05.02.01

NOC
2147, 7246

O*NET-SOC
49-2022.00, 49-2022.03

cells, its calls were switched from one cell to another by a computerized system. As long as the radiophone stayed within this network of cells, wireless communication was possible; once outside the system of cells, however, the connection was lost. After its initial tests in Chicago and Washington, D.C., the cellular network was soon duplicated in other towns and cities. As more and more areas throughout the country became "covered" with these networks of cells, it became possible to use cellular phones in more places, and the use of these phones became increasingly widespread.

In 1981, the Federal Communications Commission (FCC) announced that the wireless industry would be regulated. By FCC orders, only two competing wireless service providers could be licensed to operate in each geographic market. The FCC also announced that it would begin licensing in 306 large metropolitan areas first. Licensing in rural service areas would come shortly thereafter. As licensing got underway and cellular service was provided in more areas, the number of wireless service users grew at a rapid pace. By the end of the 1980s, there were almost 4 million cellular subscribers in the United States. By 1992, there were more than 10 million users, 9,000 cell sites, and 1,500 cellular systems throughout the country.

Also in 1992, Ameritech began the country's first commercial trials of digital wireless technology. Digital wireless technology changed the voice to numeric computer code before transmitting it, providing better sound quality and clarity than the traditional, or analog, cellular technology, which carried the voice through radio waves. Approximately 98 percent of all wireless subscribers are now using digital technology.

The wireless industry experienced a major change in 1993, when the Omnibus Reconciliation Act was passed. This legislation opened up competition among wireless providers by allowing as many as nine wireless companies to operate in a single market, instead of the two that were previously allowed. With the rapid growth of wireless service throughout the United States, there has been an increased need for qualified, trained people to manage and service the equipment. Each cell site for each wireless carrier requires constant maintenance and troubleshooting to ensure that wireless coverage is not interrupted. The responsibility for maintaining this highly important and expensive equipment is the job of the wireless service technician—a key player in the wireless industry.

According to CTIA-The Wireless Association, in 2007 there were more than 243 million wireless users in the United States.

THE JOB

Wireless service technicians are sometimes also called *cell site technicians, field technicians,* or *cell site engineers.* These workers maintain cell sites—which consist of a radio tower and computerized equipment. Each cell site covers a geographic territory that varies in size. When someone places a wireless call within a particular cell site's geographic territory, radio waves are transmitted to that cell site's antenna. The antenna picks up the radio waves and transmits them through cables to computerized equipment that is typically located in a building adjacent to the antenna. This equipment then "reads" the radio waves, turns them into a computerized code, and sends the information on to a "switching center." At the switching center, the call is transferred to its destination—which might be another wireless phone or a traditional wireline phone.

The equipment at each cell site—the antenna and computerized equipment—are important pieces of the wireless telecommunications network. If a cell site stops functioning for some reason, wireless users within that site's coverage area may not be able to use their mobile phones. Since many people rely on these devices to receive or transmit important or emergency information, a lapse in coverage can be very serious. Wireless service technicians are responsible for maintaining and troubleshooting the equipment and operations of the cell sites. The majority of cellular communication is currently voice transmissions. However, wireless service is increasingly being used to transmit data, for purposes such as Internet access. The data transmission equipment may be a separate, peripheral part of the cell site equipment, and the technician is responsible for maintaining it as well.

Diane Litchko is a technical staffing manager for Verizon Wireless. She hires employees who oversee Verizon's cell sites—called field engineer-cells. Litchko says that each *field engineer* is responsible for a group of cell sites. "Engineers are responsible for the cell site tower, the equipment on the tower, and the cell site equipment in an adjacent building," she says. "It's very complex electronic equipment."

Wireless service technicians typically perform both routine preventive maintenance and troubleshooting of equipment that has malfunctioned. Routine maintenance might include scheduled visits to each cell site to check power levels and computer functions. Technicians often carry laptop computers, which contain sophisticated testing software. By connecting their laptop computers to the cell site equipment, technicians can test to make sure the equipment is functioning as it should. Wireless carriers may also have backup equipment, such as generators and batteries, at their cell sites to ensure that even if the primary system fails, wireless coverage is still maintained. Technicians may periodically check this backup equipment to make sure it is functional and ready to be used in case of emergency. In addition to maintaining the actual cell site computer equipment, wireless service technicians may be responsible for routine and preventive maintenance of the radio tower itself and the building and grounds of the site. In many cases, technicians do not perform the actual physical maintenance on the tower and grounds themselves. Rather, they contract with other service providers to do so and are then responsible for ensuring that the work meets appropriate standards and is done when needed.

The frequency of the scheduled visits to individual cell sites depends on the technician's employer and the number of sites the technician is responsible for. For example, a technician who is responsible for 10 to 15 sites might be required to visit each site monthly to perform routine, preventive maintenance. In some cases, these sites may be very close together—perhaps within blocks of each other. In other cases, in less populated areas, the sites may be more than 20 miles apart.

When cell site equipment malfunctions, wireless service technicians are responsible for identifying the problem and making sure that it is repaired. "The engineers must isolate the problem—it could be a service outage from the weather, an equipment failure, an antenna problem, a security breach," says Litchko. "Really, anything that goes wrong with the site is the engineer's responsibility." Technicians run diagnostic tests on the equipment to determine where the malfunction is. If the problem is one that can be easily solved—for example, by replacing a piece of equipment—the technician handles it. If it is something more serious, such as a problem with the antenna or with the local wireline telecommunications system, the technician calls the appropriate service people to remedy the situation.

In addition to routine maintenance and troubleshooting responsibilities, wireless service technicians may have a range of other duties. They may test the wireless system by driving around the coverage area while using a mobile phone. They may work with technicians in the switching center to incorporate new cell sites into the network and make sure that the wireless calls are smoothly transmitted from one cell to another.

REQUIREMENTS

According to Litchko, wireless service technicians who work for Verizon Wireless are required to have at least a two-year degree in elec-

Wireless service technicians repair a cell phone tower. *(David R. Frazier, The Image Works)*

tronics or electronic technology. "It could be a technical school or a junior college," she says. "But a two-year degree is the minimum."

High School
If you are interested in pursuing a career as a wireless service technician, you should take high school classes that will prepare you

for further schooling in electronics. Physics classes will provide the background necessary to understand the theory of electronics. Because wireless service technician jobs are so heavily computer-oriented, computer classes are also excellent choices, according to Litchko. "You should have a strong understanding of computers, data communications, and Windows," she says. Other important classes are those that will provide you with the basic abilities needed both in college and in the workplace such as English, speech, and mathematics courses.

Postsecondary Training

A two-year associate's degree in a technical field is the minimum educational level needed to become a wireless service technician. Many technicians obtain degrees in electronics or electronic technology. For these degrees, course work would likely include both classes and laboratory work in circuit theory, digital electronics, microprocessors, computer troubleshooting, telecommunications, and data communications technology. Other students might opt for degrees in telecommunications management or computer science. Students working toward a telecommunications degree might take classes on such subjects as local area networks, advanced networking technologies, network management, and programming. Computer science courses might include such topics as programming, operating systems, computer languages, and network architecture. Although most wireless service technicians have two-year degrees, some may have four-year degrees in computer science, telecommunications, electronics engineering, or other similar subjects.

No matter what sort of educational background new technicians have, they have to learn about the specific equipment used by their employers. Most wireless carriers send their technicians through formal education programs, which are typically offered by equipment manufacturers. In these programs, new technicians learn the operating specifics of the equipment they will be maintaining. A new technician is usually given a smaller number of cell sites to manage when he or she first begins and may be paired with a more experienced technician who can answer questions and conduct on-the-job training.

Certification and Licensing

The International Association for Radio, Telecommunications and Electromagnetics offers certification for wireless and other telecommunications technicians. Contact the association for more information.

Other Requirements

The ability to work independently is one of the most important characteristics of a good wireless service technician. Most technicians work on their own, traveling from site to site and performing their duties with little or no supervision. "Our engineers work very independently," Litchko says. "So, they have to have the discipline and self-motivation to make their own schedules and set their own priorities." It is also important that technicians be highly responsible. "They must be absolutely reliable and dependable," Litchko says. "They are responsible for all the equipment at the cell sites, which is incredibly expensive, important equipment."

The willingness to learn and to adapt to change is another key personality trait of successful wireless service technicians. "This job is a constant learning process," says Litchko. "The technology is always changing, so you constantly need to learn new equipment. A person needs to be interested in learning and growing."

Finally, because so much of the job involves traveling between cell sites, a technician must have a valid driver's license and good driving record.

EXPLORING

If you think you might be interested in becoming a wireless service technician, you might first want to explore the basics of electronics, which you must understand to manage a key part of the technician's job. There are numerous books on electronics and electronic theory geared to various levels of expertise. Check with your high school or local public library to see what you can find on this topic. In addition, many hobby shops or specialty science stores have electronics kits and experiments that allow young people to get some hands-on experience with how electronic circuits work.

To find out more about wireless communications specifically, you might again check for books or magazine articles on the subject in local libraries. You might also contact a wireless provider in your area and ask to talk with a cell technician about his or her job.

EMPLOYERS

There are dozens of wireless service providers, both large and small, all over the United States. Anywhere that there is wireless service—that is, anywhere that you can use a cellular phone—there is a cell site, owned and maintained by a wireless provider. Some of the largest wireless providers are AT&T Wireless, Verizon Wireless, Sprint Nextel, T-Mobile, Motorola, U.S. Cellular, and Qwest. All of these companies have Web sites, and most maintain a listing of available jobs on their site.

In addition to these major players, there are smaller wireless carriers sprinkled throughout the United States in virtually every medium-sized and large community. You should be able to find a list of them by asking your local librarian for help or by doing a key word search on "wireless service providers" on the Internet.

STARTING OUT

One of the best ways to start looking for a job as a wireless service technician is to visit the Web sites of several wireless providers. Many wireless companies maintain jobs sections on their sites, which list available positions. Another possibility, according to Litchko, is to browse through wireless industry publications, such as *Wireless Week* (http://www.wirelessweek.com), *Telephony* (http://www.internettelephony.com), and *Wireless Review* (http://telephony online.com/wireless). "The industry magazines usually contain job postings, so they can be an excellent starting point," she says.

Another way to find your first wireless technician's job is to look for and attend technical job fairs, expos, or exchanges. Because technically and technologically skilled employees are so much in demand, communities frequently have events to allow employers to network with and meet potential employees. Watch local newspapers for similar events in your community. Finally, an excellent source of job leads will be your college's career services office. Many wireless companies visit schools that offer the appropriate degree programs to recruit qualified students for employees. Some companies even offer a co-op program, in which they hire students on a part-time basis while they are still in school.

ADVANCEMENT

In some companies, a natural path of advancement for a wireless service technician is becoming a *switch technician* or switch engineer. The switch technician works at the "switching center," which controls the routing of the wireless phone calls. "The switching center is the brains of the operation, which actually controls everything," Diane Litchko says. "So a switch person needs to have a broader understanding of the system, and may also have cell site experience."

Another avenue of advancement might be to move into system performance. *System performance workers* strive to maximize the performance of the wireless system. They run tests and make adjustments to ensure that the system is providing the best possible coverage in all areas and that signals from the different cell sites do not interfere with each other.

EARNINGS

Because there is such a demand for qualified and dependable employees in the wireless field, the qualified wireless technician can expect to receive a good salary. According to the U.S. Department of Labor, nonsupervisory workers employed by wireless telecommunications carriers earned a mean salary of $49,050 annually in 2006. Salaries for all telecommunications equipment installers and repairers ranged from less than $31,110 to $68,310 or more a year.

The job generally comes with other benefits as well. Many wireless companies provide their service technicians with company vehicles. Cellular phones and laptop computers, which technicians need to perform their work, are also common perks. Finally, most major wireless service providers offer a benefits package to their employees, which often includes health insurance, paid vacation, holiday, and sick days, and a pension or 401(k) plan.

WORK ENVIRONMENT

Cell site technicians who are in charge of several cell sites spend their workweek visiting the different sites. Depending on how far apart the sites are, this may mean driving a substantial distance. While the actual computer equipment is located inside a building at each cell site location, any work or routine checking of the radio tower requires outside work, in varying kinds of weather. According to Litchko, Verizon technicians are assigned a home base—either an office or one of the cell sites—from which they travel out to maintain the other sites. However, their "offices" are really completely portable: from their cellular phones and laptop computers, they can do their work anywhere. "The key is that they are totally mobile," Litchko says. "Through either phone lines or wireless connections, they can tap into the computer system at any of the cell sites. They truly live in a wireless, mobile environment."

This is important because the management of cell sites is a 24-hour-a-day, seven-day-a-week business. If an alarm system goes off at three in the morning, a cell site technician must respond. The ability to access the system remotely from his or her laptop computer may save the technician an actual trip to the site. Because the sites must be maintained continuously, wireless service technicians are likely to sometimes work unusual hours. Litchko's technicians work regular hours, for the most part, but they take turns being "on call" to handle emergencies. "How often you have to be on call depends upon the number of people on a rotation schedule," she says.

Most wireless service technicians are not very closely supervised. They generally set their own schedules (with management concurrence) and work alone and independently. They may, however, have to work closely at times with other company employees to integrate new sites into the system, make modifications to the system, or troubleshoot problems.

OUTLOOK

According to the U. S. Department of Labor, employment in the telecommunications industry is expected to grow more slowly than the average for all industries through 2016. This is mainly due to vast improvements in telecommunications equipment and the automation of system monitoring and repair.

Despite this prediction, rising demand for wireless services and the creation of new wireless networks should ensure job opportunities for workers in this segment of the industry. There are several reasons for the growing popularity of wireless service. Perhaps the most significant reason is the steady decrease in prices for cellular service. Since 1988, the average monthly bill for wireless service has gone from approximately $95 to approximately $50, according to CTIA-The Wireless Association. A second reason for the increase in usage is that coverage areas are increasingly broad and comprehensive. As more and more cell sites are added, more and more parts of the United States have cellular service. Areas that previously had no wireless service are being covered. Consequently, more people have access to and use for cellular phones and pagers. In 2007, there were 210,360 cell phone sites in the United States—more than double the number in 2000.

A third factor in the growth is the continuous improvement in cellular phones and services due to technological advances. New technologies are allowing people to transmit data as well as voice over wireless connections. Examples of wireless data communication include such applications as text messaging, videos, photographs, and Internet access.

In recent years there has also been an increase in the number of wireless companies. This growth was spurred by the Federal Communications Commission's partial deregulation of the industry in

1993, which allowed for as many as nine carriers in a geographic market. This competition has added a large number of technicians' jobs and is expected to continue to do so.

FOR MORE INFORMATION

For job postings, links to wireless industry recruiters, industry news, and training information, contact
CTIA-The Wireless Association
1400 16th Street, NW, Suite 600
Washington, DC 20036-2225
Tel: 202-785-0081
http://www.ctia.org

For information on certification, contact
International Association for Radio, Telecommunications and
    Electromagnetics
840 Queen Street
New Bern, NC 28560-4856
Tel: 800-896-2783
http://www.narte.org

For the latest on the wireless industry and job information, contact
Wireless Industry Association
8290 West Sahara Avenue, Suite 260
Las Vegas, NV 89117-8931
Tel: 800-624-6918
Email: contact@wirelessindustry.com
http://wirelessindustry.com

For information on the wireless industry in Canada, contact
Canadian Wireless Telecommunications Association
130 Albert Street, Suite 1110
Ottawa, ON K1P 5G4 Canada
Tel: 613-233-4888
Email: info@cwta.ca
http://www.cwta.ca

Index

Entries and page numbers in **boldface** indicate major treatment of a topic.